Surf-riding

Plate 1 (see overleaf). Giant surf at Sunset Beach, Oahu, Hawaii.

By Don James, Culver City, California

SURF-RIDING

ITS THRILLS AND TECHNIQUES

BY O. B. PATTERSON

CHARLES E. TUTTLE COMPANY
RUTLAND, VERMONT & TOKYO, JAPAN

Representatives

For Continental Europe:
BOXERBOOKS, INC., Zurich

For the British Isles:
PRENTICE-HALL INTERNATIONAL, INC., London

For Australasia:
PAUL FLESCH & Co., PTY. LTD., Melbourne

Published in Japan by the
Charles E. Tuttle Company, Inc.,
of Rutland, Vermont & Tokyo, Japan
with editorial offices at
Suido, 1-chome, 2–6, Bunkyo-ku, Tokyo

Library of Congress
Catalog Card No. 60–10364

First printing, 1960
Tenth printing, 1966

Layout of illustrations by Kuniko Tomoda
Manufactured in Japan

To Zaida
and my son Richard

Table of Contents

List of Illustrations

PLATES

FIGURES

Introduction

Only those who have the fortunate opportunity to witness or to acquire the art of surfing can know the tremendous thrill that comes from following the sport.

I had the good fortune to witness a surfing contest in California twenty-five years ago and immediately succumbed to its exciting thrills. I still remember the pleasure I experienced while watching those trim surfers race across the crest of mountainous walls of white water as they came charging on their boards to my very feet.

Since that time this exciting and truly Hawaiian sport has been my keenest hobby and I have endeavored to promote and to bolster its interest here and elsewhere as it spreads throughout the world. International Surfing Championships held in Hawaii each year during the Thanksgiving holidays have united surfers from many nations in friendly competition, thrilling thousands of spectators as the contestants vie for honors and victory over the challenging sea.

It is through the intense interest and assistance from enthusiasts such as O.B. "Pat" Patterson, whom I have known for the past twenty years, that this stimulating and ancient sport has gained such popularity around the world.

INTRODUCTION   Through this publication, Pat brings you first hand, many highlights of this sport of Polynesian kings. *Mahalo Nui Loa!*

1960   John M. Lind
                                             Past President, Waikiki Surf Club
                                             Co-founder, International Surfing
                                             Championships, Hawaii

14

Author's Foreword

To know fully the thrills of life one must live! Life, being identical with activity, both mental and physical, brings us to the realization that the fullness of living can only be experienced through coordination and harmony of body, mind and spirit. Such fullness of living, the surf-rider feels and knows. He gazes out over the open sea in search of mountainous waves and, on sighting one, tosses his board onto the surface of the water. Stepping onto the board with effortless sureness he soon drops full length upon its deck and with a few deep strokes into the tropical water he glides away from the shore out into the breakers that come crashing over the coral reefs. When you see him finally speeding along the surface of the wave cutting across the swollen crest like the blade of a knife, racing ahead to keep his board from being swallowed up by the ever-pursuing breaker which speeds towards the shore, you will realize that you have witnessed a superb exhibition of grace, rhythm, and co-ordination. All phases of pleasant living call for this harmonious adjustment, for without it we miss much of the beauty and happiness that comes from knowing and doing the things worthwhile.

In the field of sports, and particularly in that of surfing, infinite care is given to proper timing and co-ordination of muscular action. To maintain a proper balance on the surfboard a surfer must allow his body to relax. He must not allow nervous tension to overpower the steady flow of physical adjustment which is necessary for proper control of his board. He must be mentally alert and instantly aware of the slightest changes in weight balance, and he must look ahead to judge his anticipated action. To do all this successfully he must have complete co-ordination of his mental and physical processes. The Hawaiian surfers have an expressive and pleasant way of describing this condition. They calmly call to the beginner, "Cool head, Brudda." And a cool head it will have to be if he is to master this most exacting of sports.

If you have felt the thrill of a rushing stream driving your frail canoe downward through tossing, convulsive rapids, just missing a boulder here and a sudden turn there, then you have to some degree felt the force of action and thrill that surges through the heart of the lone surfer as he is madly driven by the constantly pursing breaker across the shimmering surface of the sea. And it is here along the broad beach stretches where in ever-growing numbers gather the followers of this sport of Polynesian kings, our modern princes of the surf.

It is hoped that this effort to present these glimpses of surfboarding adventure in the Pacific will bring the reader as much pleasure as I have experienced in exploring the subject and writing the text.

I am grateful for the courteous assistance of the Library of Hawaii where a great storehouse of rare Hawaiiana was opened to me. There it was possible to read the many legends and accounts which deal with the sport of surfboarding in past ages, and which form the source of the material contained in Part Three of this book. We regret that more space could not be allowed to give the reader further glimpses of these delightful tales and of the experiences enjoyed by the ancient Polynesians.

Sincere appreciation is also extended to a loyal friend, William C. Capp, who introduced me to this exciting sport, and who generously gave of his time when I was learning to ride my board. It was Bill who first encouraged me to write this story of surfing.

I would also like to acknowledge the assistance of my son, Richard, who as an accomplished surfer aided me in several areas of the test, briefing me very carefully on surfing features and locations.

1960

O. B. Patterson
Honolulu, Hawaii

PART ONE

SURFING AND SURFBOARDS

1. Riding Your Board

The day has finally arrived when you are going to be exposed to this, the most thrilling of sports, for the first time. This experience will automatically initiate you as a *malihini* (new) surfer. The surfboard will in due course of time, put you through one of the most thorough initiations that one could wish for, and it will be packed with thrills, embarrassing situations, and incidents that can hardly be appreciated by you until the art of surfboard riding has been mastered. At that time you can sit back self-assured on your board and observe others as they go through the discouraging and trying hours that no one can escape during the first exposures to this most exhilarating of sports.

It is our desire to assist you in every way possible in becoming adept on your surfboard by at least getting you through the first stages of the game which are responsible for many persons giving up before they have derived any enjoyment or benefit from the time and energy spent in learning it.

As you place your board in the water for the first time, do not even look out at the waves ; your primary mission is learning to paddle and steer the board with ease and self-assurance.

After reading this far, it may appear that we are trying to discourage you, but to the contrary, it is our aim, or rather method of instruction, to

21

give you as clear and complete a picture as possible so that your initiation days will be few in number and your ambition to become an expert surfboard rider achieved in the shortest possible time.

We have been "put through the mill" forward and backward by that hard-boiled teacher, experience; so if you will only be patient with us and apply yourself wholeheartedly in your efforts, we can assure you of many enjoyable days on your board, full of thrills, carefree relaxation, and humorous happenings which you will carry as fond memories throughout your life.

First you try to gain the proper position on the board. Ease up over the edge of the board, keeping your body parallel to the longitudinal axis of the board, taking up the position as shown in Plate 10. Arch your back so as to raise your chest and shoulders above the board, resting your weight upon the short ribs. Distribute your weight so that the board is in a balanced or level position laterally and the nose slightly higher than the stern. Now you are ready to take the next position. Place your hands in the water alongside of the board, as far forward as possible. Now draw them downward and to the rear, keeping the arms nearly straight and the fingers close together, but not held rigid (see Plates 8 & 10). Continue this paddling action until you have the board moving at the desired speed and that speed from which you receive the greatest amount of motive power with the least effort. The arms and hands, upon completion of each stroke, are quickly but smoothly brought forward for the next stroke. Always remember—*smooth rhythmic coordination* in the strokes will give you more power, better control, more speed and less fatigue.

After learning to paddle your board in a straight course, you are ready to practice the various ways of maneuvering while paddling. Using the arms by dragging one while working the other, or by varying the pull, will turn the board to the side on which the least power is expended.

Next you may try projecting your toes into the water alongside of the board on the desired side in which direction you wish to turn. Another method is to shift the weight of your legs on the side to which the turn is desired; preferably by raising the leg on the opposite side slightly and crossing it over to the other side.

22

Plate 2. Picking up a big wave at
Cunha Surf. At left, Conrad Canha.

Plate 3. Thrilling surf at Makaha Beach, Oahu, Hawaii.

Plate 4. Several stages of handling your
board.

By Clarence Maki, Honolulu, Hawaii

After practicing the above-mentioned methods of guiding your board, you will subconsciously begin using various combinations to best maneuver the surf board while paddling. Mastery of the art of paddling is most essential before attempting to ride the waves. It is necessary to gain considerable speed *before* the wave and then to keep the path *perpendicular* to the wave front.

When you have mastered the paddling technique you are ready to venture forth to catch your first wave. It is advisable at first, to choose small waves that have already broken so that you may learn to handle and steer the board in the prone position before attempting to stand up.

As the wave approaches, commence paddling, gradually increasing your speed to its maximum upon the instant of contact with the crest of the wave. As the wave picks the board up and pushes it forward, place your hands upon the board and shift your weight so as to keep the nose from "pearl diving" or going down, and also to turn the board from side to side, using a foot or leg on the necessary side to make correction in direction. Slight variations in fore and aft weight shifting can be obtained merely by raising yourself up and back or by taking a position closer to the board.

To go out through waves that have already broken requires practice and perfection if you wish to save time and energy. As you approach the wave head on, paddle strongly and directly into it with the nose of the board several inches higher out of the water than for the normal paddling position. Upon contact, grasp the gunwales on either side and raise the body, which will allow a considerable portion of the wave to pass between your body and the board without forcing you backwards too strongly. Using this method to go through large waves rests wholly with the strength and ability of the individual.

If you should be surprised at any time by large breaking waves which may cause you to doubt your ability to handle the board, the following method will keep you from being washed toward the shore and will also facilitate keeping the board in your possession. Turn the board about, headed for shore, sit on the stern of your board, grasp the gunwales on either side and lean back, keeping the arms extended, the legs clamped tightly against the

27

board and slightly underneath. In this position the nose of the board will be high in the air and, by maintaining that position with your back toward the wave, you will let the wave go by you. In cases where the situation becomes dangerous, shove the board free and dive in the opposite direction (see Plate 6) to avoid being injured by your own board.

Now you go out for the first ride on which you will stand up. Paddle out to a position where the waves appear to be about ready to break. Take up your position with the board headed toward shore, or slightly turned to facilitate looking over your shoulder for the wave which you want to catch. Commence paddling to gain your maximum forward velocity just as the wave catches up with you. Rise rapidly to a standing position on the board as soon as you feel the wave pick you up. Do not try getting up on one knee at a time but come smartly to a standing position with the left foot forward and the feet slightly apart, the legs and body relaxed (see Plate 19).

The fore and aft position on the board will be determined by the size of the wave and the speed. The faster you travel, the farther back will be your standing position. Carrying your weight centered too far to the rear of the board will eventually cause loss of the wave and, too far forward, will outrun the wave and the board will "pearl dive." Proper balance and shifting of weight can only come from practice and experience. There are various ways of maneuvering your board while standing. The method most commonly used is to shift the weight from one foot to the other. This of course, causes the board to turn toward the side upon which the most weight is applied. In using this method, one soon discovers that carrying the weight of the body upon the heels and transferring it from one heel to the other, as required gives the most satisfactory results.

Another method of steering that comes only after much practice is to drag the toes or a foot in the water on the side upon which the turn is desired. This is greatly facilitated by the use of weight shifting in conjunction with the dragging method. That is, to make a turn to the left you could either stand on your left foot and drag the right foot in the water on the left side by crossing it behind the left; or you could shift your right foot over to ap-

28

proximately the center of the board and drag the left foot in the water off the left gunwale.

Another means of steering but one which is not widely used, is to stoop over and drag a hand in the water on the side to which you desire to turn. This method is convenient for making slight changes in direction just after picking up a wave which has insufficient speed for effective use of other methods of steering.

After learning to steer and maneuver your board while lying down and standing up you are ready to take up sliding which is the act of maneuvering the board along the face of the wave. This will give a much faster and longer ride than progressing straight towards shore with a wave. The ideal spot to ride a wave is at the edge of the curl and to slide away from the break. That is, if you start on a swell and it commences to break on one side or the other, you turn your board away from the break and slide just fast enough to keep out of the "soup" (broken water). In this particular phase of surfing you will find that carrying and shifting your weight upon the heels secures and maintains the desired degree of speed for sliding across the wave front. Carry your weight far enough to the rear of the board so as to cause the board to ride high on the wave. Never let it run down the wave as this sacrifices much control, and you would be unable to pull over the wave in case it began to break across the entire front. If the wave breaks over, to avoid getting caught in it, step back and put your weight on the side to which you are sliding and you will find yourself safely out of it.

Much practice is required in judging the proper waves to ride and when certain ones should be passed up. Watch waves form on the horizon and learn to anticipate where they will be the best for riding and just where they will break over.

The *malihini* surfer is more or less forced to do a considerable part of his riding in waves that have broken. This gives him excellent experience in handling his board and helps him to develop the self-assurance that he will need to handle his board properly in large waves. Therefore, if you experience *pilikia* (trouble) in learning to slide your board, and, particularly, to

29

"hold" it in slide, do not immediately become discouraged. It requires regular practice and application of the fundamentals of surfing before you can get the best out of a good wave.

Whenever you are spilled or thrown from your board, always attempt to keep hold of the board and get it back under control. If you have your hands on the board, you will know where it is and it will not be hitting you unexpectedly. Also, other surf-riders will not be subjected to the dangers of a "free" board through your carelessness.

Many valuable pointers can be obtained by observing an expert surfboard rider in action, and, if you observe and study what he is doing and the results he obtains, your period of learning will be considerably shortened.

Join us in this thrilling sport:

> When the sea is raising hell
>   with breakers crashing high
> We will cheer for those brave lads
>   who dared join us and try!

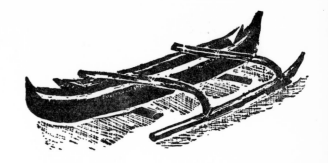

2. Building Your Board

During the past 50 years the shape of the surfboard, which began as a crude floating log, has been changed repeatedly. One of the earliest recorded Hawaiian boards weighed about 150 pounds and was hewn from a single piece of wood. In 1957, the Bishop Museum in Honolulu displayed fifteen surfboards covering a century of surfing in Hawaii. One of these collectors' items, probably the oldest surfboard in existence, was a small body-surfing board said to be several hundred years old.

There were two large *koa* wood boards also in this display weighing 148 and 160 pounds each, which were used at Waikiki by a native high chief named Abner Paki. He stood six feet four inches in height and weighed 300 pounds. Chief Paki's 160-pound board, which was sixteen feet long, was believed to have been hewn prior to his birth in 1808.

In early times there were two types of surfboards generally made in Hawaii. The *alaia* (thin) board, made of *koa* or breadfruit wood was considered to be for body-surfing. The *olo* (thick) board, a log-type such as that used by Chief Paki were generally made of lightweight wood. However, his large board described above was made of *koa* which is quite heavy but durable.

The general trend in surfboard construction since 1900 has been toward

lighter and more maneuverable boards, probably because the new genera-
tion of surfers is not as powerful as that of the giants of early Hawaii. After
the turn of the century even the natives began to use the lightweight California redwood for their boards. During this period California surfers were
developing hollow boards. Some of these craft were called "cigar boxes" by
the natives who shunned them generally. It was not until the 1930's that
balsa wood came to be used in the construction of surfboards. These first
boards were made of balsa and spruce, glued together and shaped much
like the solid redwood planks of previous years, only quite a bit thicker.
This type of California board was used successfully at Waikiki for "tandem"
surfing (two on a board). In the middle 1930's it was not an uncommon
sight to see a beach boy hoist some frightened tourist upon his shoulders
and come riding into the beach. An experience long remembered by the
tourist you may be certain.

Surfboard construction did not change too radically until the late 1940's
and early 1950's when the all-balsa board became popular both in California, where it was developed, and in Hawaii. The board was first referred
to as the "hot curl" board due to its excellent maneuverability. Due to the
great popularity of this type of board we will begin instructions with it.

California surfers encounter waves which pile up to a great height rather
abruptly and the crests of these waves move to the right or to the left rapidly. As the surfer should always ride just at the crest, he must have a type
of board that, at a second's notice, can turn sharply in either direction.

The early plank, the old hollow board, and even the laminated balsa and
spruce boards of the 1930's turned sluggishly and robbed the surfer, particularly in California, of many exciting rides. To remedy this handicap, the
California boys developed the Malibu-type all-balsa board (see Fig. 1).
These California surfers should also be credited with the development of
the new plastic coating now in common use. Prior to this time surfboards
were coated with varnish which gave poor protection to the delicate wood
required for surfboards. A slight hit from another board or even the
gouge of a fingernail could open a leak which would allow seepage of
sea water resulting in wood-rot if the leak were not promptly repaired. This

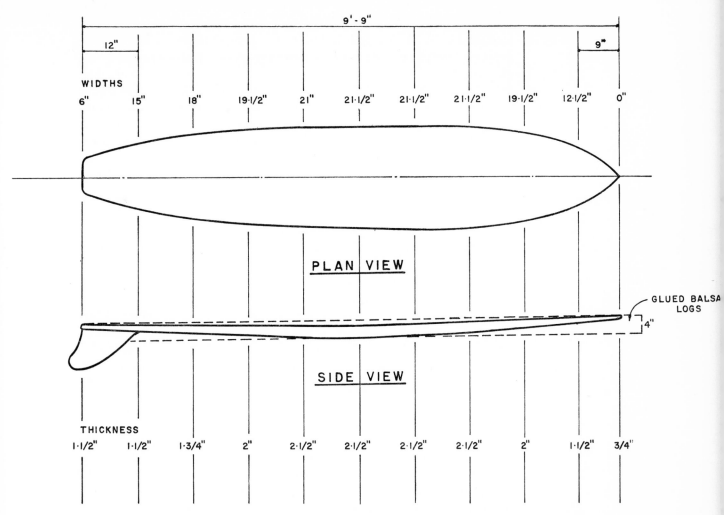

Fig. 1. Malibu-type Surfboard

33

new coating of plastic, sometimes called "skin" can resist an average hit and of course is weather resistant.

MALIBU-TYPE SURFBOARD CONSTRUCTION

Before beginning the construction of your all-balsa surfboard (see **Fig. 1**) you should locate a safe place to store your materials and in which to build your board without interference. Begin by checking all local sources of balsa wood. Each piece must be selected with care and warped or damaged pieces must be rejected. Check carefully to see that there are no rot spots in the wood. Get pieces with similar grain because the finished board will reveal the grain much more clearly than will the board in its raw wood stage. You will need four pieces four inches thick, six inches wide, and about ten feet long.

Next you should assemble an adequate number of extension C-clamps, a jack plane, drawing blade and sanding equipment. These items must be available throughout the period of construction.

Begin your work by first smoothing the edges of the balsa on the sides that are to be glued together and set them together loosely to make certain they will line up properly. Now apply your glue, (the powdered casein type) to those edges to be glued, place the pieces within the extension C-clamps, then tighten them carefully but firmly. Care must be taken to avoid too great strain on the balsa as the wood is fragile and easily damaged. Allow the assembly to set for at least twenty-four hours; then remove from the clamps, place it on a firm bench or a solid structure and carefully shape it to dimensions as shown in Figs. 1, 2, and 3. Balsa wood is very pulpy in texture and you should begin your shaping cautiously in order to learn just how to apply your plane, drawing knife blade and the sanding equipment without sustaining damage to the assembly.

You will note from the drawings there is a 1½ inch "rocker" from the tail to the nose of the board. By this we mean that the center portion of the deck is 1½ inches lower than the nose or the tail. This gives the board a slight rocker shape and improves its maneuverability on the wave.

Plate 5. Going out over the big wave and riding the curl at Ala Moana, Waikiki.

Plate 6. Diving clear of board at Sunset
Beach, Oahu, Hawaii.

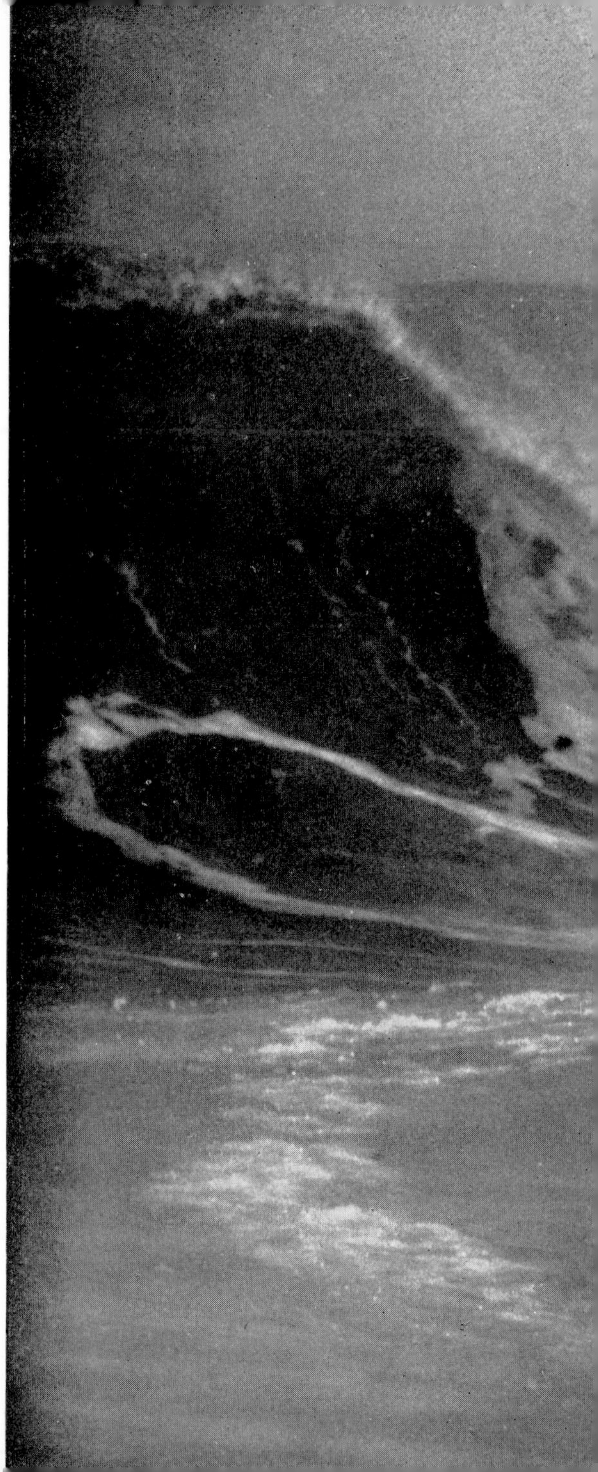

By Don James, Culver City, California

Plate 7. Sliding away from the break,
Makaha Beach.

By Scoop Tsuzuki, Honolulu, Hawaii

At this point you should shape your plywood skeg or keel and have it ready to attach to the tail of the board as shown in Figs. 2 and 3. When the finished board and skeg surfaces have been sanded to a smooth texture, your plastic must be prepared. The plastic consists of a marine resin and a catalyst is added when preparing it to vary the speed of drying. Marine supply houses furnish with each purchase detailed instructions that explain the use of the catalyst, how to apply the glass cloth next, and, later on, how to sand and finish surfaces. Apply a generous coating of the plastic to the deck. Press woven glass cloth onto this wet plastic coating, then cover the glass cloth with another coating of plastic making certain to tamp out with your paint brush all small air pockets which may be revealed under the glass cloth. With a sharp knife or razor blade, trim off the glass cloth along the sides of the board about halfway down on the gunwales between the deck and the bottom. When this has dried thoroughly turn the board over and repeat the process. The skeg is attached later. Cut long strips of glass cloth six inches wide and apply them in a like manner so that they circle the entire gunwales of the board evenly overlapping the raw edges of the deck cloth and the bottom cloth already applied. This will lend added protection to an area which is most likely to sustain damage.

After this first covering is dry, sand the surfaces smooth. The second coating of plastic is now applied to the deck. When dry, turn your board over and coat the bottom with plastic. Now, set your skeg (see Figs. 2 and 3) on the wet surface making certain it dries in an accurate vertical position and pointing precisely to the center of the nose of the board. Glass cloth should be cut or chopped up into fine particles and mixed with the plastic to form the filler that will be shaped at the base of the skeg to give it support and strength. The filler (see Fig. 3) is applied on both sides of the skeg from front to back of the skeg. It tapers out to about two inches on either side of the skeg. When this has dried, sand surfaces of the entire board smoothly and then apply your last coating to the entire board. This last coating should be sanded smoothly. The construction of your board is now completed, and you are ready to go out and challenge all concerned.

We wish to add that there are unlimited variations of shapes and lengths

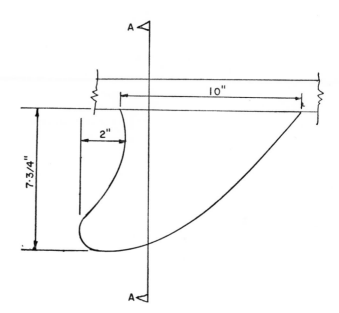

Fig. 2.

for the all-balsa type board. Each surfer has his own pet theory of the perfect board. So, for the benefit of old-time surfers we add "cool head Brudda," we didn't say this was the perfect board. It is intended as the best all-round board for the average size surfer and for use in all types of breakers.

Why don't you build yourself one of these boards and get out there and "give it a go," as the Aussies down under so aptly put it?

HOLLOW-TYPE SURFBOARD CONSTRUCTION

The hollow-type surfboard (see Fig. 4) we recommend for construction purposes is not intended for open sea waves but is primarily for use in calm seas.

40

SECTION "A" OF SKEG

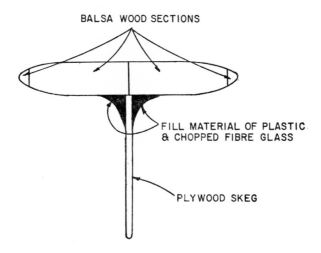

BALSA WOOD SECTIONS

FILL MATERIAL OF PLASTIC
& CHOPPED FIBRE GLASS

PLYWOOD SKEG

NOTE: APPLY LAST PLASTIC COATING OVER BOARD & SKEG Fig. 3.

This very simple and economical board is, however, an all-purpose one; though rather fragile is light in weight and can speed through open seas, over lakes and rivers with ease and grace due to its small water displacement and its long slender shape. It can be built of fairly inexpensive material, which if properly planned should cost approximately $25.00 to $30.00.

Variations of this board have been used for many years in Hawaii and California both for open sea racing and for paddling about for fun and exercise. We recommend construction of this type of board for beginners as it is very stable in the water and can be used by the entire family.

In selecting the deck and bottom material choose top quality three-ply spruce plywood, or its equivalent. It should be free of knots or blemishes.

The wood comprising nose and tail pieces (see Fig. 5) should be of good quality and the ¾-inch thick gunwales should also be made of top-quality spruce or white cedar in order to hold the many screws securely. Use 1-inch brass flat top screws for securing the deck and bottom and 2½-inch brass screws for securing the ¾-inch thick ribs to the gunwales and to the tail and nose pieces.

Begin the board by cutting and shaping the nose piece, the tail piece, the ribs and the two gunwales. The ribs should be cut to lengths that allow for the proper overall width of the board when secured to the two gunwales. The nose piece should be fitted, glued, and screwed to the gunwales first. Then begin to glue and screw the ribs to the gunwales, starting with the frontmost rib. After the last rib has been attached, set in the tail piece with glue and with 2½-inch brass screws. Secure the assembly in pressure clamps and allow a 12-hour drying period (see Fig. 5).

Throughout the construction keep in mind that this assembled craft must be made watertight. Therefore, be sure to fit all parts carefully, fill in the glue to make solid connections, and pull the pieces securely together with the screws.

The bottom should be cut to specifications in Fig. 4 remembering that it is slightly rounded and that, therefore, the plywood must be a little wider than the overall finished width of the board. Drill holes for the 1-inch screws with a drill that is much smaller than your screws. Make the holes 2½ inches apart and set in at a sufficient distance from the outer edge to grip the ¾-inch gunwales and the ribs see Fig. 5.

Cut and set the deck piece in the same manner as described for the bottom. Be sure to apply your marine type glue (powdered casein glue is preferred) freely to all surfaces that are to be drawn together by the screws. It is better to use too much than too little.

The drain plug with an air vent 1/6-inch wide drilled in its center should now be installed as shown in Fig. 4. The drain should be of brass and can be obtained at a good marine supply house at the time you get your glue, screws, and marine paint.

42

By Gordon Scott, Honolulu, Hawaii

Plate 8. Pat Patterson in a kneeling position, paddling a laminated board.

By O. B. Patterson, Honolulu, Hawaii

Plate 9. Dick Patterson at surfboard lockers, Outrigger Canoe Club.

Plate 10. Pat Patterson in a prone position, paddling surfboard.

By Gordon Scott, Honolulu, Hawaii

Plate 11. Mrs. Eva Pomeroy of Hawaii with the Walter McFarlane Memorial Trophy.

By O. B. Patterson, Honolulu, Hawaii

Plate 12. Steamboat (stern) and Curly (*man with hat*) with a load of visitors riding the wave at Canoe Surf, Waikiki.

By Clarence Maki, Honolulu, Hawaii

You are now ready to begin your sanding of all exposed surfaces. Sand all sharp edges of the board into gently rounded edges. When surfaces have been made velvet smooth, apply your first coat of marine paint on the deck area and let it dry thoroughly. (Your marine supply dealer will tell you how much time is required.) Turn your board over and paint the bottom.

The entire painted surface should be sanded smooth with fine sandpaper before adding the second coat. Two or three coats should give you the texture. The last coat should be sanded smooth also and if you have some special design or insignia, apply it on the deck to identify your board.

For those who desire a skeg (keel), a good assortment should be available at your marine store and you may refer to Fig. 5 for installation details.

FOAM SURFBOARDS

The newest idea in surfboards from California is that of the "foam" board. It is still being tested and improved, but many are in use both in California and in Hawaii.

This board has the general appearance of the Malibu balsa board and, like it, is covered with an outer skin of plastic-glass. The board is made of a new liquid called polyurethane which is poured into a mould to the shape desired. This liquid is mixed with a chemical substance which causes the liquid to foam with air bubbles when it is poured into the mould and placed under a pressure of 350 to 450 degrees. To control the weight of the finished board it is necessary to properly estimate the amount of the chemical substance in the mixture, thereby controlling the size of the air bubbles in the completed board.

When this new process was first tried, many of the boards would break under stress on the waves. The builders are now giving the boards extra strength by including balsa wood stripping on the inside.

The idea of the new foam board is to utilize a material that will not absorb sea water whenever the board is damaged. Water absorption has been the constant problem faced by all surfers who have used balsa or other lightweight wood.

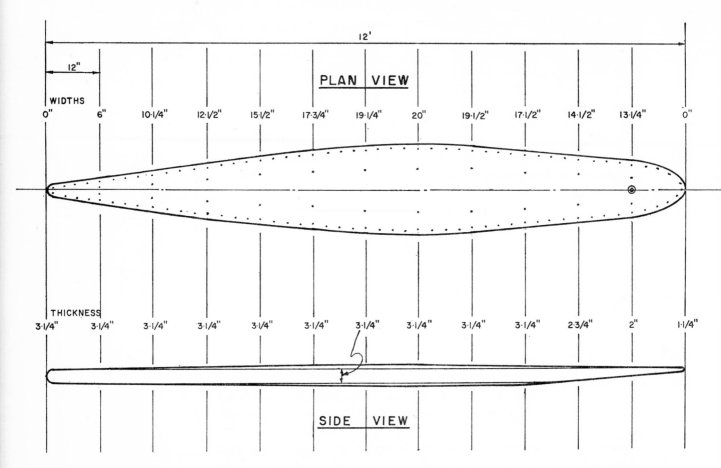

PLAN VIEW

12'

12"

WIDTHS

0"   6"   10·1/4"   12·1/2"   15·1/2"   17·3/4"   19·1/4"   20"   19·1/2"   17·1/2"   14·1/2"   13·1/4"   0"

THICKNESS

3·1/4"   3·1/4"   3·1/4"   3·1/4"   3·1/4"   3·1/4"   3·1/4"   3·1/4"   3·1/4"   3·1/4"   2·3/4"   2"   1·1/4"

SIDE VIEW

NOTE: DECK & BOTTOM ARE OVAL ENOUGH TO ACCOMMODATE RIBS WHICH ARE GRADUATED FROM 1" IN HEIGHT AT CENTER OF BOARD, TO "O" AT NOSE & TAIL.

Fig. 4.   Hollow-type Surfboard

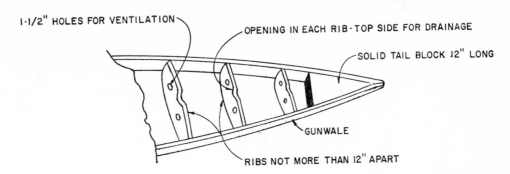

1·1/2" HOLES FOR VENTILATION

OPENING IN EACH RIB - TOP SIDE FOR DRAINAGE

SOLID TAIL BLOCK 12" LONG

GUNWALE

RIBS NOT MORE THAN 12" APART

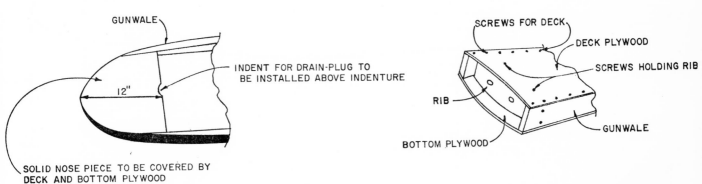

GUNWALE

INDENT FOR DRAIN-PLUG TO BE INSTALLED ABOVE INDENTURE

12"

SOLID NOSE PIECE TO BE COVERED BY DECK AND BOTTOM PLYWOOD

SCREWS FOR DECK

DECK PLYWOOD

SCREWS HOLDING RIB

RIB

BOTTOM PLYWOOD

GUNWALE

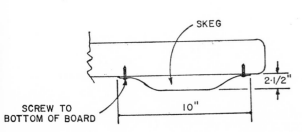

SKEG

2·1/2"

SCREW TO BOTTOM OF BOARD

10"

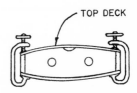

TOP DECK

INSERT SCREWS AND USE SEA CLAMPS TO HOLD FOR 12 HOUR DRYING PERIOD

Fig. 5.   Hollow-type Surfboard (details)

47

Because of the complicated procedure required for construction, these new boards originally sold for $95 to $125; however, as the process is standardized, it is possible that the boards may eventually sell for less than the balsa-type board.

SURFBOARD BUILDERS

A great percentage of the newer type boards in use today both in Hawaii and in California were made by professional surfboard builders. For those of our readers who do not wish to build their own boards we suggest that they contact any of the following listed recognized builders, or persons for information:

1. Velsy and Jacobs
   Dana Point, California

2. "Hobie" Alter
   Dana Point, California

3. George Downing, Athletic Coach
   Outrigger Canoe Club,
   Honolulu, Hawaii

4. Robertson-Sweet
   Pacific Palisades
   California

5. John Lind, President
   Waikiki Surf Club
   Honolulu, Hawaii

6. Preston Peterson, Co.
   Santa Monica Pier
   Santa Monica, California

7. Surf Shop
   2686 Great Highway
   San Francisco,
   California

48

3. Care of Your Board

The hours of pleasure that you derive from your surf board can be increased by caring for it properly. As you watch surfers ride their boards in close proximity to each other, there undoubtedly arises in your mind the question of damage to the boards resulting from collision while in motion. Actually the boards very seldom touch, and only on rare occasions are they damaged, while traveling in the same direction. Most boards receive their *pukas* (holes), splits, and various other damages as the result of "pearl diving," by not supplying a suitable storage rack in which to keep the board when not in use, carelessness in transporting by automobile, and laxity in caring for the surf board upon the beach.

The principal thing to keep in mind is that any damage to your board should be repaired immediately before more damage results from the action of the salt water upon the fibers of the wood. Allowing the unprotected wood to remain exposed to the elements results eventually in the necessity for major repairs when actually your surf board could have been repaired at very little cost and practically no loss of time or energy had it been given immediate attention. Many times the board will absorb water through exposed sections and will increase in weight. This may adversely affect its balance and riding characteristics.

A suitable storage rack is a necessity for the proper care of any surfboard. The rack may be either of the vertical (see Plate 9) or the horizontal type. Placing your board in its rack after surfing allows it to dry properly. In the case of hollow boards it is advisable to remove the plug and drain whatever water may be contained inside before standing the board in the rack. Leave the plug out while the board is stored so as to allow any additional water to drain and to dry out the inside more thoroughly; also for free expansions brought about by changes in temperature. The drain in a hollow board is at one end thus facilitating the removal of water. It is, therefore, advisable to store this type of surfboard in a vertical rack. Laminated boards which derive practically their entire longitudinal strength from the laminations may be safely stored in either type of rack or locker without any damage resulting from twisting or bending.

It is advisable to store a Malibu-type surfboard in a vertical position as it is more fragile than other boards and may be damaged more easily when lying down. When placing your board in the rack do not allow it to stand in a puddle or damp spot.

Proper care of your surfboard upon the beach is very essential, as this is one place where much damage occurs unknowingly to the average owner. It is always advisable to place your board in a vertical position whenever possible after bringing it out of the water. Never bring your board in and place it down flat upon the beach because this allows the underside to remain wet and rest in damp sand, while the upper surface dries off too rapidly. In hollow-type boards this will result in unequal expansion taking place and damage to the board due to cracking of the finish, and, in many cases, in the loosening of the glued joints. Always stand the board upon one edge, and, if necessary, to hold it in this position a small quantity of sand may be piled on either side. Examine the sand upon which the board is to be placed for sharp rocks that may injure the board. In the case of hollow boards, the plug should always be removed immediately upon taking the board from the water not only to drain the water contained inside but to allow free expansion and contraction to occur without harm to the structure.

When repairing your surfboard put the board into dry dock for a sufficient length of time to allow the damaged section to dry out completely. The length of the time required will vary according to the type of material of which the board has been constructed.

When securing wood to make repairs, it is important that the piece being replaced or repaired be duplicated in regard to density and classification. This is especially true when making major repairs requiring large replacement pieces. Any piece of wood marred by blemishes or splits should be rejected for use upon any part of a surfboard.

In making glued joints, particular care should be taken in the selection of the glue to be used. In the case of casein glue the manufacturer's specifications should be followed in detail in regard to mixing and application, with special observance of mixing instructions and the time limits pertaining to them in order to obtain the desired results. The receptacles and brushes or sticks used in the mixing should be clean and free of any glue from previous mixings. To obtain a good mixture water is added to the glue slowly while stirring rapidly, using one part of glue to two parts of water according to weight. After mixing thoroughly, the glue is allowed to stand for at least fifteen minutes before using. Casein glue should not be used until more than four-and-a-half hours after mixing.

An excellent glue that may be purchased commercially is known as Belt Cement. Mainly because of the time and procedure required in the preparation of casein glue it is recommended that Belt Cement be used except where very large quantities are required.

The first step in the repair of *pukas* (holes) in solid boards is to remove every trace of the damaged section so as to insure a smooth and firm foundation for the glued surfaces. Next, carefully cut out the replacement block with a saw, allowing approximately 1/16 inch on all sides for planing down to a perfect fit. The block should be cut to a thickness that leaves it with ⅛ inch to ¼ inch at least projecting above the surface after it is carefully fitted into the prepared place in the board. You are now ready to glue the piece into the board.

First, size both the aperture in the board and the replacement block with a thin coating of glue. After approximately five minutes apply a sufficient amount of glue to all surfaces requiring it and put the block in place. Clamps may be used if applicable; otherwise, it will be necessary to weight the repaired section sufficiently with some heavy object to hold the block firmly in place and force out all of the excess glue and air that may have collected between the surfaces that are being joined together.

Allow the glue enough time to dry before planing the inserted block down flush with the surface of the board to conform to the original contour of the board. The minimum drying time is approximately eight hours, but it is preferable to leave it overnight.

After the inserted piece has been planed down flush or nearly so with the surface of the board it should be sanded down very smoothly with the sanding operation extending for several inches on either side of the patch. Boards that are varnished (old style) are repaired with varnish. Boards that are plastic covered are repaired with plastic and fiber glass applied as described on page B4. The final step is the application of at least three coats of your varnish or plastic. After each of the first two coats has dried thoroughly, it is sanded down with very fine sandpaper in order to enable the next coat to grip the surface and to remove irregular spots or particles. The final uppermost coat is not sanded.

TRANSPORTING YOUR BOARD

Surfboards are generally transported on racks secured to the top of automobiles. The standard type rack consists of two sections one of which is placed across the top of the car just above the driver and the other placed across the car just above the rear seat. The better racks have rubber suction cups to hold and support the rack and they will not damage the paint of the car, if properly used. They occupy a minimum of space in the luggage compartment and surfers should carry them in the car at all times as standard equipment. Good racks are available at most sporting goods and department stores for as little as $8.00 to $10.00.

Always rinse your boards free of sand or dirt before storing or transport-

Plate 13. A *wahine* out of control at
Waikiki.

By Clarence Maki, Honolulu, Hawaii

Plate 14. A *malihini* in *pilikia* (trouble)
at Cano. Surf, Waikiki.

By Clarence Maki, Honolulu, Hawaii

ing them. When more than one surfboard is carried, place generous padding between the boards and make certain your straps are secured firmly to avoid loss of boards in transit. In panel trucks or station wagons, rest your boards on padding on their sides and secure them carefully. For owners of convertibles it is advisable to rest the boards across the front and back seats letting the major share of the weight rest across the back seat. Boards should not be wedged into the small trunk compartment, leaving the major part of the board suspended behind the car, unsupported.

You will observe that top surfers keep their boards in excellent condition. So, for your own satisfaction, resolve to keep your board in good operational repair at all times and you will never be caught "on the beach" when the "big ones" start to roll!

PART TWO

*SURFING
TODAY*

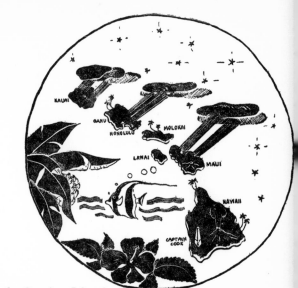

4. Surfing in Hawaii

Many of the earliest proficient surfers came from the lovely Garden Island of Kauai. Kauai lies approximately ninety miles to the northwest of Oahu and enjoys a somewhat cooler climate. This island is, geologically, the oldest of the entire group. Tropical forests blanket the Waimea Mountain Range. Viewed from the air, one can see silver waterfalls hurtling a thousand feet into the blue Pacific leaving snowy mists of spray framed by brilliant double rainbows of reflected sunlight.

The ancient kings held court and lived principally at Waimea where they could be close to the sea and could fish and swim in the clean bays and lagoons nearby. The bays are fringed by the ever present coral reef, and many of the reefs throw the swells up in such a manner as to afford just the necessary surge for daring surf board riding. Kauai did not mother any weaklings when she spawned her surfing children. She gave them speedy waves and a thrilling sea to drive them perilously through the surging swells and shimmering sprays, into the calm waters that wash the white sands of her broad beaches.

Hawaii, the island of belching volcanoes and the restless fire pit of Kilauea, is next in importance when we consider the ancient Hawaiian locations for surfing. As well as being the most weu-known it is by far the largest island of the group, with an area of 4,030 square miles lying about 190 miles southeast of Oahu.

Although Kauai possibly developed earlier surfers, Hawaii is distinguished as the great benefactor of the sport of surfing. The first water and surf carnivals were held at Kealakekua Bay on the west coast of Hawaii and many legends recall exciting adventures in connection with the surfing carnivals, showing that contestants were sent from all the islands to participate in the sport.

The reef at Kona on the west side of the island of Hawaii did not afford constant surf; however, when the sea was high, brave men challenged each other and were either defeated by the sea or rewarded by an exciting ride to the shore.

The Valley Island of Maui is close to the hearts of all Hawaiians who know her. It is just a little larger than the island of Oahu, having an area of 728 square miles. Her name, Valley Island, was earned because of the mild and fertile valley that lies between the mountains of Haleakala and Puu Kukui.

Maui has never laid claim to supremacy in surfing or in surfing locations, but her men have many times shown their ability in this sport. She has many legends dealing with surfboarding and outrigger sporting on her ancient pleasure coast known as Hana. It was here that her royal families loved to spend happy days fishing, swimming, and basking in the surf. More recently, surfing activity has grown at Wailuku where there is a sweeping bay just inside the coral reef. A recently constructed sea wall has almost spoiled the bay for surf, just as a similar wall ruined the surf at Balboa in California. However, Maui still enjoys the sport and many boards may be seen daily gracefully skimming the water with their riders.

The island of Oahu with her world-famous beach at Waikiki is of course considered the home of surfboarding activity. Legends speak of surfing activity in the present harbor of Honolulu where the surf was known as "Ke Kai o Mamala" (the Sea of Mamala). Kou (the ancient name for Honolulu) was the gathering place for sporting events, *luaus* (feasts), and carnivals.

60

Surfing was not as hazardous here as at locations by other islands. Many women frequently participated. Waikiki Beach in the old days was too far from the indulgent, festive center and, therefore, was not often frequented. However, with the awakening of commerce through contact with the whaling ships, Honolulu began to attain commercial prominence; and with the sudden growth of harbor business and general city development, there grew a desire to find a more agreeable and peaceful resort. Court life remained in Honolulu but resort life and sporting activity moved out about five miles to the shady palm groves of Waikiki. Here the Hawaiians were able to enjoy a variety of surfing activities because of the different kinds of surfs depending upon the seasons of the year.

At this time surfing activity never really made any great progress in technique at Waikiki, but rather tended to become a little tame. This was due partly to the gentleness of the Waikiki surf most of the year. There are, however, occasional accounts recalling individual accomplishments during high surf.

The swan song for surfing came to Waikiki when the missionaries arrived in the 1820's and took charge. But of far greater interest, the rebirth of surfing came entirely at Waikiki after 1900. We believe the coming of the missionary *haole* (white) to be the cause of the lost interest in surfing and the tourist *haole* years later to be the stimulating spirit behind the revival of this great sport. At least we can safely say that the tourist now supports to a great degree, praises, and publicizes surfing, and through him many outside countries have heard of or adopted this most thrilling of sports.

When we speak of surfing in Hawaii we feel we must include canoe surfing because both the canoe and the surfboard are used to ride the same waves and in many instances canoe captains are top rate surfboard men. The sport in Hawaii embraces both the board and the canoe in much the same way as in Australia where it has been said that in a single hour probably 10,000 persons may be seen enjoying the rough-and-tumble surf waves on surf skis, in the rugged lifesaving surf boats, or on a variety of surfboards.

Canoe racing has been gaining in interest since World War II and there are now numerous events staged annually. These events are invitational and some of them are as follows:

Labor Day Races at Waikiki
Territorial Championships
Maritime Day Races
Kamehameha Day Races
Walter J. McFarlane Memorial Races (see Plate 11)
Koolaupoko Lions Races at Kailua

The Outrigger Canoe Club has recently added a number of fiberglass all-fabricated canoes to its fleet. These canoes were built by the O.C.C coach, George Downing. A very kind Hawaiian lady, Mrs. Eva Pomeroy (see Plate 11) has blessed each one of these canoes according to the traditional Hawaiian custom in which the canoe is placed down at the water's edge and draped with sweet-smelling flowers. Then a prayer of blessing is chanted in Hawaiian, and a fresh husked coconut is struck against the bow so that the milk christens the new canoe. These fabricated canoes are built in the same size and shape as the standard *koa* wood log canoes; however, they are much lighter and are far more economically maintained.

In the past hundred years Hawaii has experienced occasional high seas resulting from earthquakes or tidal waves which, it is said, were accompanied by waves forty to fifty feet in height. In researching some of these records we find a few accounts of very dramatic rescues and some amusing incidents concerning the use of improvised surfboards.

During the tidal wave of 1868 when the waves were said to reach fifty feet we learn that one native, finding himself and his house being swept to sea, yanked off a board and used it as a surfboard to reach shore.

A dramatic and heart warming sea rescue occurred some years ago during a storm on the north coast of Oahu when a surfer on the beach spotted a man far out to sea. Not having a surfboard at hand the brave lad yanked off a cottage door, tossed it into the churning sea and rescued the unfortunate swimmer.

A tidal wave alert was sounded on the island of Oahu in 1957 and residents were warned to leave the beach areas. If you know any surfers I am

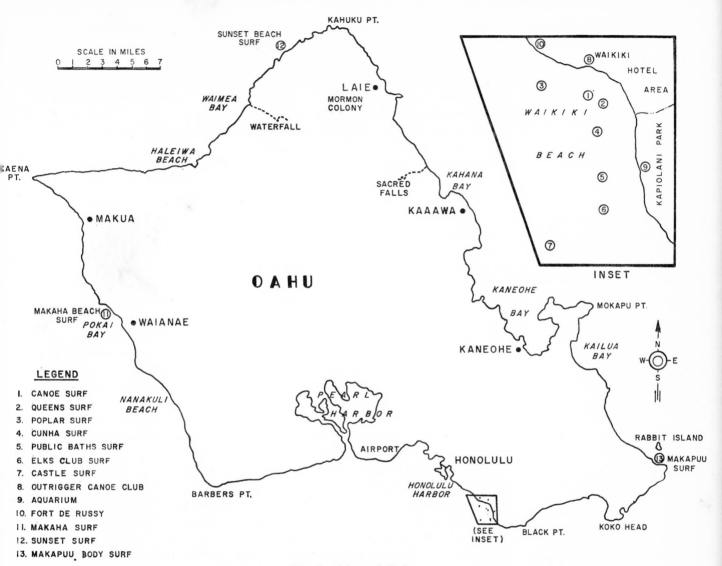

Fig. 6. Map of Oahu

SCALE IN MILES
0 1 2 3 4 5 6 7

KAHUKU PT.

SUNSET BEACH
SURF ⑫

WAIMEA
BAY

LAIE ●
MORMON
COLONY

WATERFALL

HALEIWA
BEACH

KAENA
PT.

SACRED
FALLS

KAHANA
BAY

KAAAWA ●

● MAKUA

OAHU

MAKAHA BEACH ⑪
SURF   POKAI
BAY

● WAIANAE

KANEOHE
BAY

MOKAPU PT.

KAILUA
BAY

KANEOHE ●

N
W ─ E
S

LEGEND

1. CANOE SURF
2. QUEENS SURF
3. POPLAR SURF
4. CUNHA SURF
5. PUBLIC BATHS SURF
6. ELKS CLUB SURF
7. CASTLE SURF
8. OUTRIGGER CANOE CLUB
9. AQUARIUM
10. FORT DE RUSSY
11. MAKAHA SURF
12. SUNSET SURF
13. MAKAPUU BODY SURF

NANAKULI
BEACH

PEARL
HARBOR

AIRPORT

BARBERS PT.

HONOLULU

HONOLULU
HARBOR

(SEE
INSET)

BLACK PT.

KOKO HEAD

RABBIT ISLAND

⑬ MAKAPUU
SURF

INSET

⑩

⑧ WAIKIKI

HOTEL

AREA

③

① ②

WAIKIKI

④

BEACH

⑨

⑤

⑥

⑦

KAPIOLANI PARK

63

sure you will realize what they did. These "iron men of the sea" simply went down to Waikiki grabbed their surfboards, paddled out, and waited for the "big one" to arrive. However, when the water began to slip away from under them and they realized they were standing on the ocean bottom, we are happy to report that instead of waiting for the "big one" they had planned to ride past the Royal Hawaiian Hotel and up Kalakaua Avenue, they instead dropped their boards and rushed posthaste for high land!

HAWAIIAN SURFING LOCATIONS

The island of Oahu with its famous beach at Waikiki Bay is the present world capital of the thrilling sport of surfboarding. As we have seen, in ancient times the Polynesians of old Hawaii surfed at many locations; however, only in Waikiki Bay (see Plate 16) has this sport been pursued consistently over the past fifty years. It is here that it was finally rejuvenated by the natives and by a few *haoles* who were Hawaiian at heart!

There are six major locations on the reef that fronts on Waikiki Bay where surfboarding is regularly enjoyed. Of these, Canoe Surf (see Plate 16) enjoys the greatest number of surfers daily. This location is in the very heart of the bay in front of the Moana Hotel, about 500 yards from Waikiki Beach. Here you will see great numbers of newcomers learning to control their surfboards. One must begin some place and, as this is the handiest spot, it draws most of the beginners. As a result of this gathering of would-be surfers, the area just between the good waves and the beach has become known as the "bone yard." Many are the bones bruised or broken in this area when beginners tangle up in masses of loose boards. The loaded outrigger canoes utilized for passenger purposes constantly ply their trade through this "bone yard" and of course this tends to make a good show for the wide-eyed tourists in the canoes. They have come to Waikiki to live dangerously, and some of them do! Now, let's get back to telling about surfing locations.

The more agile surfers, and particularly the daring ones, prefer to paddle out to Poplar Surf. This surf is located about twice as far from the beach, out in front of the Reef Hotel one-half mile nearer Honolulu. Here you will see the recognized surfers who are masters of their sport.

Another excellent surf location is Queens Surf. This is located nearest to the beach just in front of the Biltmore Hotel and is used almost entirely by the younger native boys. This surf breaks very fast and the slide is a "tight" one to the right and very thrilling while it lasts.

The three remaining major surf locations in Waikiki Bay are for the strong in heart, be they Polynesian or *haole*. These locations are commonly called Cunha Surf, Public Baths-Elks Club, and Castle Surf. The longest, fastest, largest, and most magnificently challenging surf occurs in these areas which are all located in the same general vicinity.

In his youth the beloved Duke Kahanamoku and some of his buddies frequently picked up breaks out nearby Steamer Lane and played their boards through Big Castle, Public Baths, and Cunha Surf, and then raced in to land their boards upon the sand at Waikiki Beach! This represents a distance of well over two miles of battling the sea breaks. Although the surf runs high in these areas only a few times a year, when it does, the strong at heart are still bewitched by it and they will lock up their shops or play hooky from their jobs and will put on a magnificent surfing show for the natives and tourists alike. Of course if you wish to see them as they first catch the wave far out at sea on the horizon (see Plate 15) you will need to have field glasses handy.

Although Waikiki Beach is synonymous with surfboarding, there are other surfing locations on the coastline many miles from Honolulu. The most popular of these locations is about forty miles west of Honolulu and has become known as Makaha Beach. Here the surf frequently runs high and here the annual International Surfing Meets are held.

This area has been a favorite location of California surfers who have migrated to the Paradise of the Pacific. Many such migrants have taken up their residence in the area, or keep their scant belongings and surfboards in a converted panel truck or an old, battered station wagon. They live as near to the water as possible, especially when the surf is running high.

Some of these automotive contraptions are amazing to behold! They are crammed with refrigeration, gas stoves, and strange sleeping racks, and it is not too surprising to hear the buzz of an electric shaver drifting out through a makeshift porthole or window. These vehicles are works of unlikely imagination painted like Jacob's coat, if painted at all, and one wonders as to their ability to move themselves on the highways.

In its present phase of development Makaha Beach is rapidly becoming a colony of San Onofre nomads transplanted from California. Many appear to be in search of the good life where dinner is cooked over an open fire on the beach, where dishes are washed in the sea, if at all, and where the informal life of the colony just drifts out into the clear blue moonlight. You may hear the strains of an occasional ukulele, listen to the most amazing yarns, particularly about the big ride someone almost got, or you might enjoy an impromptu hula gracefully executed by a native girl who just happened to be passing by in the night.

First Break Surf at Waikiki (see Plates 17 & 24) runs only on rare occasions. It was very popular with the old-timers who surfed in Hawaii in the 1930's. A distinct disadvantage now is the fact that the good First Break waves lead the rider to crowded Canoe Surf which is often used for practising by large numbers of newcomers to the sport. However, First Break Surf is near enough to the major hotels in Waikiki to be viewed by the many visitors; and on a good day this area will furnish them with some very exciting scenes to remember because, whenever First Break is running, the other surfing spots in Waikiki are usually getting excellent surf and great numbers of top surfers will be scattered across the bay, waiting at *their* own preferred spots for that "biggest wave of the day."

One of the newest surfing spots in Waikiki is located between Kaiser's Hawaiian Village Hotel and the new Honolulu Yacht Harbor. When the present deep harbor entrance was recently dredged through the reef, the ocean currents and reef were altered in such a manner so to set up a new surf. This known as Ala Moana Surf (see Plate 27) and is rapidly becoming popular with many of the experienced, transplanted California surfers,

66

Plate 15. Beginning the ride at Castle
Surf, Waikiki.

By Clarence Maki, Honolulu, Hawaii

Plate 16. A telescopic view of the big waves at Waikiki Bay.

1a, 1b, 1c : Canoe Surf
2 : Blowhole Surf
3a, 3b : First Break Surf
4 : Cunha Surf
5 : Elks Club Surf
6 : Public Baths Surf
7 : Papanui Surf

Plate 17. Blue Makua riding First Break
Surf at Waikiki Beach.

By Clarence Maki, Honolulu, Hawaii

some of whom park their panel trucks in which they live just on the jetty immediately in front of this surf, and need only toss their boards into the harbor and paddle out when the surf begins to run.

Let's now move on to the largest surf in the Hawaiian Islands. This surf is called "Sunset" and is about thirty-five miles north of Honolulu (see Plate 26). Here the surfer is seldom seen. Only when the sea is stormy do the breakers build up in a manner where surfers have a chance to use surfboards. Heavy surf in this area generally has a dangerous rip tide running through it. When the "big ones" are running here, they may reach a height of 25 to 30 feet and it is said that only fools go out to try!

It is strange how word gets passed on when the "big ones" come. Who knows, maybe it's the *menehunes* (tiny legendary people) who speed the glad tidings. One thing is certain, when the "big ones" do come, so do the dedicated surfers and the show is on!

Waimea Bay on the north side of Oahu, has always been considered a dangerous place for the swimmer. Only within the past few years have surfers tried to use their boards here and most of these have been California boys. On December 16, 1958, two of these California surfers, Jim Caldwell and Rick Grigg, were in a group of surfers trying to pick up 20-foot waves. They lost their boards and in an attempt to assist each other, were finally stranded out beyond the heavy breakers. Firemen from the town of Waialua and a helicopter from Air-Sea Rescue were summoned to rescue them. Just before dark, the firemen, on surfboards and with ropes tied around their waists, helped them the last few hundred yards to shore. Wise Hawaiian surfers usually give this place plenty of respect.

SURFING ORGANIZATIONS IN HAWAII

It is not likely that early Polynesians enjoyed any particular types of organized fraternal groups attempting to share jointly such pleasures as surfboarding or canoeing. The ancient Polynesians lived much as a tribe of early Americans, sharing their food as well as their superstitions and their

71

pleasures among themselves in small bands. These bands were ruled by chiefs who were worthy of being chiefs because of their physical strength and courage, and because of their inheritance of rank. There was no honorable place in the tribe for a weakling and certainly no place in the household of a chief for any signs of inferiority; therefore, in order to command and hold authority the leaders diligently schooled themselves in courageous activity.

In the field of combat, they were the boldest and most courageous, and in their pleasures they were equally dauntless being as bold as lovers as they were warriors. In their search for the thrill of living they developed hazardous sports such as hill-sliding and surfboarding. The narrow grass-covered, elevated slides built to reach the mountain tops, drove the long sleds toward the sea at a terrific speed equal to that of the flying surfboard, and only the brave hearts and superior strength of the chiefs could instigate such daring (see Fig 9).

To these early masters of their people belongs the honor of developing the sport of surfboarding. It is not difficult to imagine some powerful, young giant of the chief's household standing upon his beloved beach looking out to sea, watching the growing swells as they approached the coral reef, and suddenly being charged with a desire to conquer them just as his household had conquered all its foes. To this first adventurous and ingenious man of courage and spirit we raise our glasses in deep appreciation.

Many years passed and during this interval surfboarding grew in interest and overshadowed all other Polynesian sports. During this period there were no clubs, but there was a unison of spirit which showed itself in the inter-tribe and inter-island surfing carnivals which were regularly held throughout the Hawaiian island group. It was not until the rebirth of surfing activity following the turn of the present century that groups of young sportsmen began feeling the desire to band together in friendly groups to enjoy surfing and to challenge others for recognition of superiority in this activity.

One of the first individuals to personally encourage and supervise the

72

forming of a fraternal group was Duke Kahanamoku. It all began to evolve when the Duke was about fifteen years of age, back in 1905. Some dozen of the youngsters who spent much of their time at Waikiki sitting out on their boards "shooting the breeze," or, more often, sitting under the largest *hau* tree resting, suddenly decided to give themselves a name. They called themselves the Hui Nalu (group together waves) boys and in future years they met at this largest of all *hau* trees, much as the mainland kids met at the "ole swimmin' hole." When the Outrigger Canoe Club established itself at Waikiki there were three able competitive fraternities to immediately challenge them; the Hui Nalus, the Myrtles, and the Healanis. As is always true in sports, competition served to refine and solidify their spirits, and thus came into being some of the leading groups that still enjoy worthy recognition in water sports.

The Outrigger Canoe Club which was established May 1, 1908, was the first club to provide proper facilities for the encouragement of surfing. By 1910 they had built a spacious grass hut for the storage of surfboards and canoes just at the water's edge at Waikiki Beach. It was their desire to have a place at Waikiki where the young men of the town could change their clothes, participate in beach sports and meet socially.

The club's purpose was to perpetuate and foster aquatic sports, particularly that "sport of Kings" surfboard riding, as well as outrigger canoe riding. From its beginning of a humble grass hut, bought from the zoo in Kapiolani Park and re-erected on the club grounds, the club has grown in membership and popularity, until today it is known round the world.

In the past the club fielded football teams, rowing crews, track teams, volleyball, basketball, and swimming teams, and has sponsored or supported sailing and canoe regattas, surfboard competition and other sports, winning a wealth of beautiful trophies.

Basically a beach club, it has become a meeting place for many tourists as well as town people who are being entertained by the club members. For many years it has included among its members a large number of both young and old surfers, most of whom learned to surf there when very young.

73

Its greatest interest today is the perpetuation of surfing and canoeing; and its some 2,000 members either participate actively in or promote these great sports.

The famous Beach Patrol which is operated by the club is under the very able direction of the internationally known surfer George Downing. He is Club Coach, Master Canoe Builder and holder of many national records in surfing competition. This patrol is composed of top rate beach boys who make a very lively and lucrative living instructing visitors in the art of swimming, surfing and canoeing. They furnish much of the native color that is so long remembered by the visitor. Such hallowed names as "Colgate," "Panama," "Chick," "Frank," "Splash," "Keakona," "Molokai," "Sally," "Brains," "Pau," and "Tough Bill" will always revive fond memories in the minds of visitors and residents alike, who have enjoyed their company and happy hospitality. The boys possess a high sense of honor and have been constantly entrusted with the care and instruction of tiny children and aged persons alike. They are no more impressed by VIP's than by a child, and the VIP's like it that way!

Intrepid surfers are not found exclusively in any one club or organization. A good representation does come from the vicinity of the Outrigger Canoe Club but an equal number can be also found in the vicinity of the Waikiki Surf Club. Watchmakers, lawyers, grocers, bankers, executives, and truckdrivers all answer the call from a "pal" who tells them the "big ones" are running. Of such men are surfers made!

After the turn of the century, Hawaii enjoyed many visits from European royalty, diplomats and other prominent persons, and records indicate that, almost without exception they all wanted to try their hand at surfboarding at Waikiki. Surfing seems to have caught their imagination and pointed to a thrill they did not want to miss. We are told that Duke Kahanamoku and his worthy buddies were usually on hand to offer assistance and encouragement.

Many individual feats of endurance have been recorded from these early years, and probably the greatest was that performed by Gene "Tarzan" Smith when, in 1939, he paddled his hollow board from the island of Oahu

74

Plate 18. Rabbit Kekai and friend riding Makaha Surf at Oahu, Hawaii.

Plate 19. Mud Werner and Tom Zahn
at Public Baths Surf, Waikiki, Oahu.

to the island of Kauai, a distance of almost 100 miles. He made the crossing entirely alone, without assistance and without navigation guidance.

From 1939 on, civic organizations in Hawaii began to realize the importance of surfing to the community and they began to lend assistance and encouragement to surfers of all races. The first formal organization was the Hawaiian Surfing Association which was organized through the efforts of John Lind, a young fellow who had moved to Hawaii from Long Beach, California. This association did not survive World War II as the beaches were greatly restricted during the war.

Following the war the Hawaiian Canoe Racing Association was organized to direct canoe meets. This association serves a very good purpose and has representation from the major clubs in the state of Hawaii as follows:

From Oahu: Kai Oni Canoe Club, Waikiki Surf Club, Hale Auau, Hui Nalo, Healani and Outrigger Canoe Clubs.
From Hawaii: Kai Opua Club, Kamehameha Club.
From Molokai: Holomua Club.

Through the efforts of the Hawaiian Canoe Racing Association, canoe races are organized and staged throughout each year. The longest and most grilling race is the annual six-man canoe race from the island of Molokai to the island of Oahu, a distance of about forty miles over open sea. The fastest time for this crossing was set in 1957 when the Kai Oni Canoe Club crossed the finish line in five hours and fifty-six minutes. In 1958 the Waikiki Surf Club won and Kai Oni came in second. This race is held over the same route taken by King Kamehameha I when he brought his warriors in great war canoes from Molokai and conquered the island of Oahu in 1795.

The International Surfing Championships have been held at Makaha, on Oahu, each year since 1953. The meet was originally sponsored by the Waikiki Surf Club and the Waianae Lions Club. However, in 1958 the Lions Club withdrew and the Waikiki Surf Club, after four months of determined planning sponsored the entire meet which proved to be the most successful one held to date. The last day of the four-day meet drew more than 15,000 spectators.

Past champions at these Makaha meets are as follows:

1954

Senior Men: George Downing
Junior Men: Allen Gomes Jr.

Senior Women: Not scheduled
Tandem: Walt Hoffman and Joan Jones

1955

Senior Men: Rabbit Kekai
Junior Men: Allen Gomes Jr.

Senior Women: Ethel Kukea
Tandem: Ed Whaley and Nancy Boyd

1956

Senior Men: Conrad Canha
Junior Men: J. Raydon

Senior Women: Ethel Kukea
Tandem: Robert Krewson and Kehau Kea

1957

Senior Men: Jamma Kekai
Junior Men: Timmy Guard

Senior Women: Vicky Heldreich
(no tandem event held)

1958

Senior Men: Peter Cole
Junior Men: Joseph Napoleon

Senior Women: Marge Calhoun
Tandem: Rabbit Kekai and Heidi Stevens

Peter Cole from Malibu and Marge Calhoun from Santa Monica California have the distinction of being the first "outsiders" to dethrone the Hawaiians and capture the top Hawaiian surfing crowns. Their outstanding performance commanded the respect and admiration of all contestants. Peter was pressed hard to win by "Buffalo" Keaulana, Rabbit Kekai and Ricky Grigg. He stated he was able to win because the Hawaiians were

78

good sports, giving him plenty of surfing-room. A very beautiful Hawaiian *wahine,* Miss Kehau Kea, was queen of the 1958 meet.

1959

Senior Men : Wallace Froiseth	Senior Women : Linda Benson San Diego, California
Junior Men : Paul Strauch Jr.	Tandem : Ed Whaley and Diane Moore

1960

Senior Men : Richard Keaulana	Senior Women : Wendy Cameron
Junior Men : Eric Romanchek	Tandem : Mud Werner and Robin Gregg

WAHINE SURFERS

An increasing number of *wahine* (women), are taking up the thrilling sport of surfing. As previously indicated Hawaiian women in the past frequently surfed with the men and occasionally became well known for their prowess in the sport.

In recent times, Cesily Cunha of Honolulu, Pat Barker from Kauai, Pam Anderson of Waikiki, Violet Makua, an outrigger canoe captain for Waikiki Surf Club, and Mrs. Ethel Kukea of Honolulu, should probably be considered the most outstanding of *wahine* surfers in Hawaii.

Wahine surfers in Peru include Senta Eberl, Sophia Pinillos, Dora Pinillos, Karla Eberl, and Tita Berckemeyer. The Peruvian sporting circles have adopted the sport and many prominent families are represented there.

We have not personally heard of proficient *wahine* surfers in Australia; however, it is not likely that sportswomen down under are any different than elsewhere and that certainly they also must be joining their men in the sport.

5. Surfing in California

Every true surfer at some time during his career secretly longs for a pilgrimage to Waikiki, the true Mecca of the "sport of kings." However, Hawaii is seriously challenged for this honor by gallant surfers on the Pacific Coast. Their challenge in no way detracts from the glory of Hawaii and her surf, but it does seriously endeavor to match or surpass the numbers of surfers who are magnetically drawn to her shores to enjoy the thrill of conquest, and to feel the surge of the board dancing across the face of her magnificent waves.

California, that never-never land where almost everything seems to be done on a stupendous and gigantic scale, has excellent surfing beaches along a coastal expanse of over 350 miles. It has been said that more than 1,500 dedicated surfers follow the sport there both in summer and winter.

The southern outpost of the California surfer is known as Silver Gate Surf, at the entrance to San Diego Bay. This surf is large on many occasions and visiting Hawaiians say it reminds them of their Castle Surf outside Waikiki Bay.

The northernmost surf is located at Santa Cruz about a hundred miles south of San Francisco where there are a number of excellent surfers including the well-known Van Dyke brothers. To hear them tell it, the surf at Santa Cruz is beyond compare. Being so far north, one wonders how they could possibly stand such cold water. Those California thrill chasers— give us Waikiki!

We will identify only a few of the more popular surfing locations in California which are regularly used by the more experienced and enthusiastic surfers.

CALIFORNIAN SURFING LOCATIONS

Malibu Area. Because of its proximity to the most heavily populated area of Southern California, the surfing locations along the Malibu Coast annually draw the greatest number of surfers. Malibu Beach is located about thirty miles north of Los Angeles on U.S. Highway 101, and is internationally known as the playground of movie stars. Surfers are not particularly interested in this movie colony; the appeal that lies in this section is that of accessibility to good surfing breakers, and a clean beach.

A favorite meeting ground of both beginners and professionals, the surf at Malibu Beach attracts all types of surfers during the summer months. The beginners find areas suited to their abilities and the professionals take over the surf that is higher, and where the break is of the "curl" or "hook" type. These waves offer skilled surfers an opportunity to enjoy a "clean slide" provided beginners are not practising on the surfs nearer the shore. The beach, itself, presents a half-circle appearance and will accommodate hundreds of fans who decorate the sand with colorful tents, fancy towels, surfboards, and, unfortunately, a variety of litter from castoff hot dog wrappings to occasional empty beer cans.

At Malibu you will see surfboards of an infinite number of shapes and sizes. Each surfer has his own idea of the features which he must have in *his* surfboard. Many of the boards are the product of "do-it-yourself" efforts and clearly indicate creative talent, even though such a board often fails to perform to its inventor's satisfaction.

Here you may enjoy watching many of the boys clowning on their boards, standing on their heads, riding seated backwards, or with their best girl

81

riding "tandem" (standing, one in front of the other). Many such attempts end in near disaster, especially when the wave unexpectedly throws the performer off balance. We have seen this frequently happen to the great delight of the spectators on the beach who set up a rousing applause.

The water in California is far colder than in Hawaii, and the California surfers find it more comfortable to paddle on their knees (see Plate 8). This form of paddling is common at Malibu as well as at most other surfing spots along the coast.

Topanga Canyon Surf, located in the Malibu area is small and the beach is rocky at low tide. The surf resembles Malibu Beach Surf but presents a challenge to even the most expert surfers. It is good for a "right slide" of about a hundred yard's distance.

Other good surfing spots near the general area of Malibu include State Beach at Santa Monica Canyon, Sunset Beach at Sunset Boulevard, County Line at the Los Angeles-Ventura County line, the Rincon which is located at Rincon (see Plate 28) near Santa Barbara, and Point Dume, north of Malibu Colony.

The Cove. The Cove (see Plate 37) is situated at the base of a precipitous mountain, reaching to a considerable height and bearing the old Spanish name of Palos Verdes. Roads circle the mountain at several elevations and here are discernible great numbers of parked automobiles, with occupants gazing down, entranced by the small match-sized figures that go dashing about in the waves.

The beach at the Cove is narrow and comes to an abrupt end against a sheer palisade. The palisade serves as a windbreak and helps divert the often chilling winter winds from the rugged surfers as they huddle around beach fires at its base.

This fine surfing spot is only about sixteen miles from Los Angeles, but it is one of the most difficult places to reach because the surfer must carry his board and gear several hundred yards down a steep pathway to the surfing beach. This spot is used by a great many surfers but is not overrun by the type of spectators that Malibu generally accommodates.

82

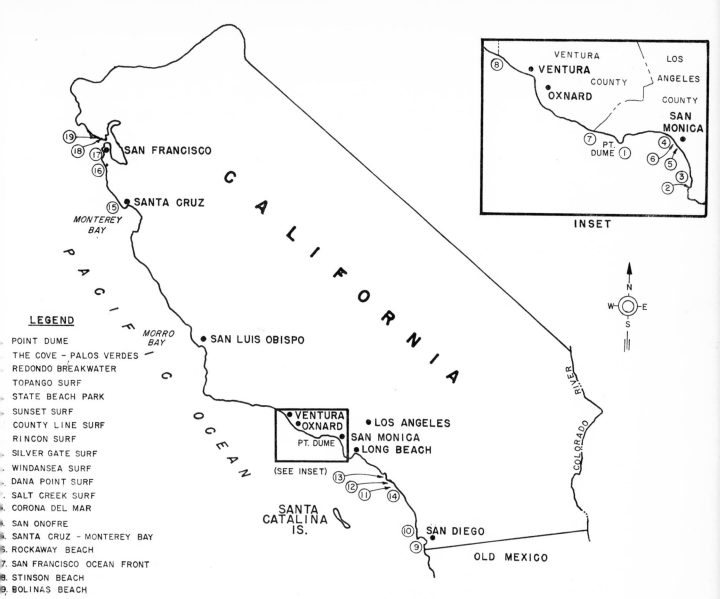

LEGEND

1. POINT DUME
2. THE COVE - PALOS VERDES
3. REDONDO BREAKWATER
4. TOPANGO SURF
5. STATE BEACH PARK
6. SUNSET SURF
7. COUNTY LINE SURF
8. RINCON SURF
9. SILVER GATE SURF
10. WINDANSEA SURF
11. DANA POINT SURF
12. SALT CREEK SURF
13. CORONA DEL MAR
14. SAN ONOFRE
15. SANTA CRUZ - MONTEREY BAY
16. ROCKAWAY BEACH
17. SAN FRANCISCO OCEAN FRONT
18. STINSON BEACH
19. BOLINAS BEACH

Fig. 7. Map of California

83

Hawaiian surfers speak well of the surf at the Cove and often compare it with surf outside Canoe Surf at Waikiki.

San Onofre. About thirty years ago surfers in California began to search for out-of-the-way spots where they could enjoy surfing and not be overrun by curious crowds. Happily, they stumbled upon an excellent surf which piled up on a reef about four miles south of the town of San Clemente, located on U.S. Highway 101 leading to San Diego.

The beach lies at the base of a rugged cliff where one may gain a magnificent view of six or seven lines of surf breaking at once, appearing as sparkling streamers being drawn across the water from the beach outwards hundreds of yards to sea.

The beach cannot be seen from the highway which crosses the elevated heights nearby, and the entrance road leading to the beach is fairly obscure; but all experienced surfers easily find their way. The entire area is a part of the Camp Pendleton Marine Base and access to the beach has been gained through an agreement with the base commander.

The San Onofre Surfing Club which was organized a few years ago has a fairly active membership of from 400–500 persons who are followers of the sport of surf-riding. We understand this is the only beach surfing location in California where entrance is said to be permitted only to the members who hold cards and windshield stickers for passage through the Marine sentry gate which secures the beach from use by the general public.

The surfboard most generally seen at San Onofre is of the all-balsa Malibu type, a little over ten feet long, three-and-a-half inches thick, weighing from 25–30 pounds and is similar to our drawings in Figs. 2, 3, and 4.

Old-time surfers have long considered San Onofre the most ideal of California surfing spots and Hawaiians who have been transplanted to California are often seen there with their surfboards. This location claims to be the surfing capital of the West Coast and rightfully so (see Plate 34).

Due to its more ideal weather, being only about seventy miles north of Mexico, the beach life is quite similar to Hawaii. Facilities of the club in-

Plate 20. *Keiki* (child) on wave at Waikiki Beach.

Plate 21. *Keiki* surfers, Waikiki Beach.

Plate 22. International Surfing Meet, Makaha Beach.

Plate 23. *Wahine* surfers of the Waikiki Surf Club at Waikiki Beach.

clude rest and dressing rooms, informal grass-type shacks for social comfort, and surfboard storage facilities. Its members hold *haole luaus* and tog themselves in true Hawaiian style. Many linger for long weekends, **living** the leisurely life of the nomad.

Other good surfing spots in the southern part of the state include Dana Point, just south of San Juan Capistrano, an old Spanish Mission town; Salt Creek, near Laguna; and Wind-an-sea, near La Jolla (see Plate 35).

Many years ago Corona Del Mar, near Balboa, was the leading surf spot and it was here that Hawaii's famed swimmer, Duke Kahanamoku, first introduced the sport of surfboarding to the astonished California sports enthusiasts.

The Redondo Breakwater Surf is a fast and fairly short ride but it is consistently good and many surfers are regularly attracted to the spot. The wave formation near the breakwater is said to be caused by a large submerged water-disposal pipe leading from the nearby power plant out to sea.

Northern California. For daring action and sheer foolhardiness we doubt if there is anything in the world that will compare to a bunch of wave-happy Northern California surfers in the act of riding the "big ones" that roll in their rugged coast. In addition to shattering waves, they must brave bone-chilling water most of the year.

In order to enjoy more comfortable year-long surfing most of them have been wearing thermal barrier suits made of special foam neoprene like the U.S. Navy frogmen use. The suit is tailored to body measure and fits like a thick outer layer of skin, without appreciably restricting body movement and blood circulation. Some of the suits reach from the ankle to the neck, with arms bare up to the shoulder tops (see Fig. 7). However, the Bermuda short or Makaha-type short is probably the most popular with surfers in the San Francisco area. Some of them have even devised a hood, boots and gloves that can be worn for more protection when they are engaging in water sports.

Unless you have tried the ocean water of Northern California, all this

87

Fig. 8. Thermal Barrier Suit

gear may sound strange, but, Brother—just take a dip for yourself and you will understand their problem!

In case you may desire to know more about this kind of gear you may write to the Surf Shop, 2686 Great Highway, San Francisco, California and I am sure Jack O'Neill will be happy to provide the necessary information.

For several years now San Francisco surfers have been scouting the entire coast line from Santa Cruz to the Oregon state line. They have found waves from 15 to 45 feet high that have tempted them, but at the present time Bolinas Beach and Stinson Beach in Marin County just north of Sausalito are the ones most regularly being used for surfing.

San Francisco Ocean Front has good surfing spots at the following places:

Kelly's Cove, near the famous old Cliff House; VFW, at the VFW hall, west end of Golden Gate Park; Roberts, at the foot of Sloat Boulevard.

San Mateo County locations are Rockaway Beach, just south of Sharp Point, and Pedro Point.

Monterey Bay has several places where surf may be found to satisfy the most daring of surf-riders. As most of the spots in this area are beyond the abilities of the beginner, the ambitious would-be-surfers usually get their sea legs at a place known as Cowels. The more seaworthy surfers in the area are known as "cliff surfers" because they usually choose Steamer Lane or North Swell. Here they must somehow get down over a very rugged cliff and either throw their board from the cliff and dive in after it or dash into the water between waves in order to make it in one piece. There are blow holes and rocky coves everywhere and many surf boards are smashed when the waves are running high. If they lose their boards here it may mean a rough swim of a half mile or more in order to recover what is left of the board. The waves at River Mouth are particularly good in the wet winter months because the sea and river build up a sand bar near 25th Avenue at Santa Cruz, resulting in larger waves than usual. The three other surfing locations in the general vicinity of Santa Cruz are Little Wind-an-sea, Pleasure Point, and Wild Hook, all with challenging names that give some idea as to the surf that may be expected.

SURFING ORGANIZATIONS IN CALIFORNIA

Just before World War II, when surfing had firmly caught the fancy of the California boys, clubs sprang up all along the coast. Most of these clubs became inactive during the war and at the present time the sport is promoted primarily by such organizations as the Los Angeles County Lifeguards; Cabrillo Beach Guards, Malibu Santa Monica Lifeguards, Venice and Huntington Beach Lifeguards, and the San Onofre Surfing Club.

Invitational surfing and paddling meets are regularly held at several locations along the West Coast, the most popular meet being the Santa Catalina Island to Manhattan Beach surf board paddle race over a distance

89

of thirty-two miles of open sea. The first surfboard crossing to Catalina was in 1933 when Tom Blake, Preston Peterson, and Wally Burton paddled from the Cove at Palos Verdes to Santa Catalina Island. Since 1955 the annual Catalina Island paddle board meet has been sponsored by the Manhattan Beach Chamber of Commerce. It has become an official A.A.U. athletic sports event and draws a tremendous following on the Pacific Coast.

Surfers from Hawaii enter this competition as well as surfers from all points along the West Coast. The Chamber of Commerce representative furnishes the boards and supervises the program for the stock paddle board event. The individually owned racing boards are entered in the "open class" competition.

The 1957 meet was held on August 26th, and the winner of the paddle board event was Tom Zahn with a new record time of six hours and thirty-eight minutes for the thirty-two-mile paddle. Mike Bright won the open class racing board event. Tim Guard of Hawaii entered this race for his first attempt and placed in the paddle board event.

In the 1958 race the first three contestants in the stock board division all broke Tom Zahn's record. Charles Reimers of Santa Monica won with a time of six hours and ten minutes. In the open class Tom Zahn again won with a new time of five hours and twenty-nine minutes and was pushed hard all the way by Jim Piper.

As in all sports, good competition results in improved form, new time records, and, of course, a constantly increasing following. Competitive events in Northern California are run between Farallone Islands and San Francisco, a distance of thirty miles. Jack LaLanne was the first to win the Surf Shop perpetual trophy on September 26, 1958, with a fast time of nine hours and twenty-two minutes against a difficult north current and adverse weather conditions.

The Surf Club of Northern California is located at 3518 Wawona Street in San Francisco and interested parties should contact it for information on surfing activities in the area.

90

Plate 24. Dick Patterson about to be "wiped out" by the wave at First Break Surf, Waikiki.

Plate 25. Wally Froiseth, Dick Patterson, and Conrad Canha at Public Baths, Waikiki, Hawaii.

Photo by Clarence Maki, Honolulu, Hawaii

Plate 26. Beating the break at Sunset
Beach, Oahu, Hawaii.

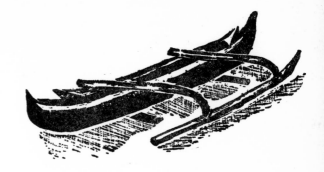

6. Surfing in other Countries

It was in February, 1915, when Duke Kahanamoku and George Cunha traveled from Hawaii to Australia to participate in the New South Wales Championship Swimming Meet, that the Australians had their first sight of real Hawaiian surfing. The Duke took his surfboard from Hawaii and gave the Australians a thrilling show which sparked the interest in surfing in that country.

Australians have long realized the value of the surfboard in practical lifesaving work. The surfboard is used by many of their leading clubs in actual rescue work and has proven to be most efficient because of its speed and control, providing a quicker and safer rescue to those who find themselves in difficulty in the surf. This contact with surfboards in rescue work has caused many of the swimmers and guards of Australia to succumb to the thrill of surfboard riding as a sport; and today we find that surf-riding is a highly esteemed sport at many beaches in New South Wales and Victoria.

Because of the particular formation of the reef along the shores of New South Wales and Victoria, many beaches in these areas offer favorable swells and breakers for surfboarding. Sydney has taken its place as the center of this activity, and stores of that thriving metropolis now offer

95

surf boards in a surprising variety—surf skis (see Plates 32 & 33), boats for the surf, and many other types of surf equipment. Eight well-known beaches offer good seasonal surf within twenty-five miles of Sydney.

We regret that so little is known to us of actual surfing activity in Australia. However, we do recognize a striking similarity in the spirit and enthusiasm of surfers of Hawaii, America, and Australia. We have learned, to some extent, of their surfing activity through our contact with prominent surfing men of Australia who have visited Hawaii and America; and through them, as well as through publications furnished by the Surf Life-Saving Association of Australia, we have learned of and greatly admire many Australians prominently connected with this "king of sports."

At Bondi Beach such men as H. Nightingale, J. Cox, and A. Hart are recognized as early great surf board riders; also, at Maroubra Beach, T. Fahey and W. Kember; at Bronte Beach, F. Adler; at South Narrabeen Beach, J. Miller and R. Tanner of Cronulla, and D. Lechleitner and H. Hutchins of North Cronulla for their great surf-riding skill. From Palm Beach, New South Wales, one-third of the way around the world from our own Palm Beach, Florida, and a considerable distance down under, we recognize K. Russell, K. Hunter, A. Major, and Judge Adrian Curlewis, president of the Australian Association of Surfing Clubs, still a fine surfer. We have listed these names at the risk of slighting many others that are possibly as worthy, but whose names are not at present available to us.

Australia's world-renowned surf lifesaving teams have been traveling from America to Africa, sharing their acknowledged proficiency in their worthwhile project. Her beaches are perhaps the most dangerous and her surf men the most daring. Hawaii first viewed her lifesaving team before World War II and following the war they were invited to return and train the local Hawaiian team. The Hawaii Surf Life Saving Association endeavors to apply the Australian methods and in 1956 sent a team to the Melbourne meet primarily to learn firsthand of the phenomenal performance of the Australians. The Hawaii team consisted of ten members including Peter Balding, Tom Zahn, Tom Moore, Tommy Shroeder, Harry Shaffer, and Danny De Rago.

96

With the introduction of the newer lighter surfboards in Australia there has been a very marked increase in surfing activity there. By 1958 most of the older cigar-box-type boards had gone and the surfers were dashing about on the crest of the wave just like the boys from California or Hawaii.

They have a very fine shop run by a Mr. Wood in Sydney for making these new boards. We have seen movies of his boards and they appear to be beautifully constructed.

LIMA, PERU

Representatives of the sport of surfboarding in Peru include Herbert Rickkets and Dr. Guillermo Weise, both of whom participated in the International Surfing Meet at Makaha in Hawaii in 1955.

Peru held its first International Competition Surfboard Paddling and Surfing Meet in 1954, and, as previously stated, Hawaii was ably represented, and her surfers royally entertained by the Peruvians.

The Club Waikiki at Miraflores, Lima, Peru enjoys an international reputation and incidentally is one of the fifty or more outstanding world clubs affiliated with the Outrigger Canoe Club of Honolulu. This club has been a staunch supporter of surfboarding and many of its members enjoy their holidays in Hawaii.

The Peruvian Consular representative for Hawaii, Mr. Neil Ifversen is a capable water sports enthusiast who has been seen almost daily at Waikiki Beach for the past twenty years. He is an experienced outrigger canoe captain and prefers the Australian water ski (see Plate 32) for surfing in the waves.

The Peruvian surfers use a large hollow-type surfboard. The light weight all-balsa surfboard has not become too popular as yet.

Surfing in Peru enjoys the support of many prominent persons including Senor Enrique Prado, the internationally known industrialist and financier. Enrique is a frequent visitor to Hawaii and a most enthusiastic supporter of the sport of surfing in his own country.

Hawaii sent a delegation of surfers to the 1957 International Competition Surf board and Paddling Meet held in Lima during March of that year. Mr. Carlos Dogney, president of Club Waikiki in Lima extended the delegates two weeks lodging as guests of his club during the meet. Hawaii representatives for the 1957 meet were Conrad Canha, "Rabbit" Kekai, and Ethel Kukea, the outstanding woman surfer of Hawaii.

In July, 1959, Club Waikiki of Lima, Peru, sent a delegation of four of their top surfers to compete in the Peruvian Invitational Surfing Meet held at the Outrigger Canoe Club on the beach at Waikiki in Hawaii. Rabbit Kekai of Waikiki Surf Club took the blue ribbon senior men's event. Richard Fernandidi and Carlos Rey of Peru placed 2nd and 4th in the event for men over forty years of age.

DURBAN, NATAL, SOUTH AFRICA

Durban, which is a surprisingly modern city (see Plate 31), is located on the southeastern tip of South Africa facing Madagascar.

Surfing enthusiasts at Durban organized the South Beach Surf Board Club in the early 1950's. South Beach is the best surfing spot in the area and we learn that surfers have been riding the waves there for several years.

The surf board was originally introduced in Durban by a visiting life-guards team from Australia. The board they took to Durban was very long and heavy and it performed well on the larger waves there at South Beach. Recently a new type ten-foot board with skeg (see Plate 30), was introduced there and supplements their older 14-to-15-foot boards used in past years.

During heavy seas there are said to be 25-to-30-foot waves at a nearby beach known as "Vetche's." We have seen some fine pictures of surfers in action at Durban, with as many as seven surfers riding simultaneously. From what we have been able to learn, great daring is required to ride the pounding breakers in that area, especially when the big surf is running.

98

In 1959, two of the more avid African surfers, Charlie Kennedy of Durban and Luke Van Wyk of Capetown sailed their thirty-foot yawl "Kudu" 14,000 miles to compete in the Hawaiian International Surfing Championships. They left Capetown in February and arrived in Honolulu late in November only a few days before the meet.

In this way surfboarding interest is growing internationally and new development in board construction as well as improved surfing techniques are exchanged and passed along.

MEXICO

One of the newer parts of the Pacific Coast to be scouted by surfers is that of the Mexican coast. In 1957 Mr. and Mrs. Greg Noll drove down the coast and located some excellent surf at Mazatlan, about 600 miles south of Douglas, Arizona. Mazatlan is located on the Tropic of Cancer and the climate there is typically sultry.

We have seen the excellent pictures taken on this trip and the waves were very impressive. The surf is located at the edge of the city and Greg Noll must have given the natives quite a start when he first paddled out and, to their amazement, began riding the waves!

The waves are long and build up to an excellent height for handling the board. They crest like the waves at Wind-an-Sea near San Diego, reaching about 10 to 15 feet for a long ride to the beach. One disadvantage is the rough rugged shore line, making it hard to get in and out without damage to the board or to oneself. Generally, the right slide is better at this location.

About 200 miles further south Mr. and Mrs. Noll located a good surf spot at San Blas. This surf was not quite as high as Mazatlan, generally, but at times it did reach a greater height. Greg had somehow passed the word back to the States and of course promptly found himself being crowded on the waves, as is usual for good surfing location anywhere.

This place is about on a latitude with the Hawaiian Islands and the country has wonderful coconuts and lush vegetation including plenty of banana groves. The boys found that a left slide was required in order to get the best and longest rides.

No doubt many more very fine surfing beaches are waiting to be discovered down Mexico way and now that Greg has opened the door it won't be long before the Southern California boys in particular will be teaching the Mexicans how to have a whale of a good time in their own surf.

7. World Surfing Greats

We have found that in the past few years, surfers from many points throughout the world are becoming acquainted with each other and are familiar with such great names in surf as Tom Zahn, John Lind, and Preston Peterson; and, to a man, they all know our beloved Duke Kahanamoku.

The authors wish to acknowledge some of the persons generally considered "surfing greats." Space does not allow a complete listing of all persons who have become prominent in this sport; therefore, we are pointing up only a few of the many fine men whom we feel have made an outstanding contribution by their boldness and courage as well as those who have, over a period of time, brought wide recognition to this most thrilling of sports. We feel it entirely appropriate to begin with a truly great Hawaiian.

Duke P. Kahanamoku.   Even if we so desired, we could not avoid heading this list with the name of our beloved Hawaiian, Duke P. Kahanamoku. The Duke has been an active surfer for the past fifty years. He is still a magnificent figure and a worthy representative of his race.

The Duke represented Hawaii in early international Olympic meets and has traveled the world representing many worthy causes. He is an internationally known Shriner, a member of the Honolulu Rotary Club, a lifetime member of the Board of Directors of the Outrigger Canoe Club and holds the office of sheriff of the city and county of Honolulu.

The Duke to us will always be Mr. Surfer!

Charles K. "Panama" Baptiste. How could one possibly conjure up dreams about surfers in Hawaii without almost immediately seeing that infectious grin on the face of Charles K. "Panama" Baptiste! To thousands of visitors "Panama" will always be Mr. Waikiki. Over the years we have watched him entertaining his friends (the visitor is his friend in four-and-three-quarters minutes) and never has he had an equal or even a near rival as a genial companion.

With the surfboard, he is one of the greatest. It's hard to tell whether he or his visitor is having the most fun. Fat ladies or little kids all seem to fall into a sort of trance under his "casual" touch. Here is a gentleman surfer; and here is a real rough and tumble surfer when he is out with the boys and the visitors are safely tucked away on the beach!

Thomas C. Blake. Tom is a renowned California surfer and designer of surfboards. He brought to Waikiki the first hollow-type board that was accepted by experienced surfers. This early board was sixteen feet long and weighed about 100 pounds. Tom later developed a sixty-pound hollow board which proved to be fast and sturdy and remained popular until World War II, when it began to lose its popularity.

Tom travels about a great deal and, although he is a California boy, he has spent several years in Hawaii and is widely known there.

Sam "Steamboat" Mokuahi. "Steamboat" is a splendid Hawaiian (see Plate 12) who is properly nicknamed. He is as calm as a lake, sturdy as a rock, and gentle as a kitten.

What a magnificent picture he makes standing like a relaxed giant, on his board as it cuts through the biggest waves. His great physical weight buries the surfboard deep into the sea and holds it "steady-as-she-goes."

102

Plate 27. Sliding left at Ala Moana
Surf, Waikiki.

By Clarence Maki, Honolulu, Hawaii

Plate 28.   Tom Zahn surfing at Rincon near Santa Barbara County Line.

Plate 29. *Keikis* and *wahinis* surfing near
Malibu Beach.

We often think of the huge statue of King Kamehameha the Great down at the Old Palace when we see him standing so relaxed and at the same time appearing so very impressive.

"Steamboat" has raised his family at Waikiki. "Steamboat Jr." is a carbon copy of this handsome Hawaiian surfer and we have reason to believe he will live up to his Dad's fine reputation in the sport of surfing.

George Downing. George is a world champion surfboard paddler and winner of the International Surfing Senior Championship for the years 1954 and 1955. He also won the six-mile Diamond Head race on December 26, 1955, setting an almost unbelievable time of forty-six minutes twenty-three and three-tenths seconds. He went to Lima, Peru, in 1954 where he won honors, and in 1956 he paddled in the Catalina Island-Manhattan Beach race, a twenty-six-mile course.

George, who has been a surfer since he was able to swim and has made water sports his career, is now serving as coach for the Outrigger Canoe Club at Waikiki.

Gene "Tarzan" Smith. Of all the transplanted California surfers "Tarzan" has accomplished the most fantastic feats of performance. An experienced surfer at the time, he came to Hawaii in the middle 1930's. His great strength and excellent physique earned him the nickname of "Tarzan" and he has certainly lived up to it.

In the 1930's he regularly paddled his board out of Waikiki Bay into Steamer Lane and disappeared from sight, just for the pleasure it gave him. During these years, as we previously mentioned, he paddled to the island of Molokai in November 1938 and later to the island of Kauai, almost 100 miles away. Although others have paddled to Molokai, none have attempted to match his crossing to the island of Kauai.

John W. McMahon. Johnnie is a transplanted California boy who has been surfing for forty years, starting his career in Venice, California. He moved to Hawaii in the year 1936, where he is now a successful business man.

He is also a daring surfer, very adept at maneuvering his board for long and exciting rides. Upon his arrival in Hawaii he immediately took to the surf and became one of the boys. With his heavy tan he is often happily mistaken for a *kanaka*.

Johnnie is still at his peak in surfing and is seen daily at Waikiki, ready to grab his board and hit the surf whenever it's "running good."

Wallace G. Froiseth. "Wally" (see Plate 25) is a real champion, especially when the waves are breaking out in the big surf. He grew up at Waikiki and has always been more intimate with the young islanders of all races than with the more pretentious surfers. Wally lives across the island from Honolulu but the word usually reaches him and brings him running when especially good surf is breaking at any point on Oahu. He is a modest and sincere man but we know of no one in the Waikiki area who has been so greatly admired by natives and *haoles* alike, over such a long period of years. Wally is still at his peak in surfing skill and it is with pleasure that we include him here.

Tom Zahn. In some ways Tom Zahn resembles the Gene "Tarzan" Smith of 1936. He is a powerful surfer and is undaunted by the magnitude of a challenge. Like Tarzan, Tom conquered the thirty-six-mile paddle to the Island of Molokai in October of 1953, with a time of nine hours and twenty minutes, and then went back to California to win the Catalina-Manhattan Beach race over a course of some thirty-two miles.

Tom has been an enthusiastic supporter of international competition and has made many staunch friends in California and Hawaii (see Plate 19).

Waldo Bowman. Of the group of surfers who were active during the thirties and forties, it is our opinion that Waldo stood at the top. He always presented a splendid picture when riding his board. His grace and intre-

108

pidity still command respect and admiration from his surfing associates. He is always a gentleman and considerate of others even when jockeying for position on the crest of a wave.

Waldo is still seen regularly at the surfing beaches and we suspect his engineering duties may at times be somewhat of a handicap, especially when he hears that big ones are running at First Break (outside Canoe Surf).

Walt Hoffman.   Walt has made many trips to Hawaii over the years since he started surfing in California. Considered one of the younger "old-timers" in California surfing circles, Walt participated in the International Competition at Makaha in 1955 and 1956, and won many honors away from the younger entrants. He is still at his peak and follows the sport loyally.

John Lind.   Johnnie has been surfing since he was a small boy at Long Beach, California. He came to Honolulu in 1937 and for the past twenty years has been a "doer" with his talents in the field of organization; and, through his persistent efforts, rules and systematical methods have been brought into use. Johnnie's surfing correspondents are scattered throughout the world, from Tel Aviv in Israel, Durban, in Natal South Africa, to Australia, Peru and California.

Through Johnnie's efforts the Waikiki Surf Club was organized in 1947. This club embraces members who could not afford membership in the existing sports clubs or who for various reasons were not eligible. The Waikiki Surf Club is truly the surfers' club, entirely dedicated to water sports and mutual comradeship. Almost immediately this club began to win honors away from the older clubs and today they field some of the finest surfing and canoeing teams in the world.

Johnnie was the first surfer to successfully campaign for the establishment of international competition. As president of the Waikiki Surf Club he was able to enlist the support of the Waianae Lions Club, and together these two organizations have staged the International Surfing Championships at Makaha since 1953. By 1954 he had successfully encouraged the Club Waikiki at Miraflores, Lima, Peru, to hold their own contest which was known as the International Competition Surfboard Paddling and Surfing Meet. Australia followed and now Durban, Natal, is inviting all champions to come and surf with them.

Internationally known and held in high esteem by all who are devoted followers of the sport, Johnnie is its tireless supporter, and is, as an individual, a fine sportsman and person.

Lorrin "Whitey" Harrison. "Whitey" was one of the first California surfers to come to Hawaii and join the Hawaiians in the "big surf." He is still a loyal devotee of the sport and attended the 1957 International Meet at Makaha.

Harrison makes his home near San Onofre and divides his interest between avocado farming, skin diving, and surf boarding. He is internationally known and has been a water sports enthusiast for almost forty years.

Preston Peterson. We believe that Peterson is probably the smartest and most capable underwater and open sea sportsman in the Pacific today.

He has had years of experience as a moving picture stunt man performing daring feats as a double for movie stars, is a professional fisherman and is still at his peak in surfing. He is the creator of the "trick tandem" surf board feature used at present day surfing meets, and taught this very difficult type of riding to Walt Hoffman. Trick tandem riding requires the surfer to ride a wave with a *wahine* either on his shoulders or in any of a great number of acrobatic poses, all performed while his board slices across a steep wave.

Peterson builds surf boards for special feature racing, for lifeguard organizations, and for general wave surfing, annually turning out a great number of superior boards at Santa Monica.

We would like to go on with these brief biographies of those whose names are a byword in this sport of kings. But space considerations compel us to

By Scotty, South Beach, Durban, South Africa

Plate 30. Reginald C. Blunt with new Australian board at Durban, South Africa.

Plate 31. Surfing at Durban, Natal, South Africa.

By Reginald C. Blunt, Durban, South Africa

Plate 32. Neil Ifverson with two-man Australian surf-ski, Waikiki Beach.

By O. B. Patterson, Honolulu, Hawaii

By O. B. Patterson, Honolulu, Hawaii

Plate 33. Dick Patterson with one-man Australian surf-ski, Waikiki Beach.

restrict ourselves at this point to a comprehensive list of names of persons, many known in surfing circles. Even so it has been impossible to include all the outstanding surfers active today ; and we hasten to add that there is no intended slight to anyone we have been unable to include in the following list.

NORTHERN CALIFORNIA

Jose Angle
Tom Berges
Dave Devine
Dave Dyc
Jim Fisher
Charles Grimm
Ray Herrick
Sam Hiona

Clif Kamaka
George Kovalenko
John Kwartz
Mike Lewis
Rod Lundquist
Dave Mojas
Jack O'Neill
Ted Pearson

Waldo Resinic
Jonny Rice
Eddy Ukini
Fred Van Dyke
Peter Van Dyke
Bill Wilson
Mike Winterburn

SOUTHERN CALIFORNIA

Ray Beatty
Fred Beckner
Jim Blattau
Bruce Brown
Mike Bright
Jim Carter
Cornelius Cole
Peter Cole
Bill Coleman
Bing Copeland
Dick Davis
Phil Edwards
Ricky Gregg

Dave Heiser
Hap Jacobs
Bill Jensen
James Lewis
John McFarlane
Mickey Minose
Greg Noll
John Pate
Walt Phillips
Joe Quigg
Charlie Reimers
Dave Rochlen
John Sieverson

Bob Simmons
Pete Simmons
Micky Shapen
Bob Shepard
Jack Sporgo
Rick Stoner
Dick Taylor
Buzzie Trent
Dale Velzy
Tom Volk
Steve Voorhees
Dewey Weber

HAWAII

Doug Ackerman
Woody Brown
Conrad Canha
William Capp
Bobbie Ah Choy
Chick Daniels
Elmer Lee
Sammy Lee
Jerome Ling
Spalsh Lyons
Clarence Maki
"Blue" Makua
Toots Minvielle
Bob Muirhead

Wilfred Godbold
Alan Gomes
Tim Guard
Tommy Haines
Sally Hale
Fred Hemmings
John McMahan Jr.
Wayne Miyama
Joseph Napoleon
Pat O'Conner
Francis O'Sullivan
John Parks, Jr.
John Parks, Sr.
James Pflueger

Richard Kauo
Sarge Kahanamoku
John D. Kaupiko
"Rabbit" Kekai
Bobbie Krewson
Richard Keaulana
Henry Preece
Richard Silva
Jits Tabata
Ed Wahley
Willy Whittle
Terry Woodall

WOMEN OF THE U.S.A.

Pam Anderson
Mozelle Angel
Pat Barker
Nan Beckner
Linda Benson
Marge Calhoun
Vickie Flaxman

Cesily Cunha
Robin Gregg
Betty Heldreich
Vicki Heldreich
Cynthia Hemmings
Pat Honl
Joan Kalahiki

Jane Kaopuiki
Kehaulani Kea
Ethel Kukea
Violet Makua
Anona Naone
Marjorie Phillips
Keala Stibbard

WOMEN OF PERU

Tita Berckemeyer
Karla Eberl

Senta Eberl
Dora Pinillos

Sophia Pinillos

MEN FROM OTHER NATIONS

Edwardo Arena, Lima, Peru
Fernando Arrarte, Lima, Peru
Augusto Barrios, Lima, Peru
Cesar Barrios, Lima, Peru
Fredrico Block, Lima, Peru
Reginald C. Blunt, Durban, Natal, South Africa
Leon "Dux" Coetzee, Durban, Natal, South Africa
Adrian Curlewis, Sydney, Australia
Barry Edwards, Durban, Natal, South Africa
Richard Fernandidi, Lima, Peru
Alfredo Granada, Club Waikiki, Lima, Peru
Charlie Kennedy, Durban, Natal, South Africa
Ken C. Lindsay, Livermore, N.S.W., Australia
Phipip Nel, Durban, Natal, South Africa
Fernando de Osma, Lima, Peru
Arthur B. Parkyn, Mooloolaba, Queensland, Australia
Dorian Paskowitz, Tel Aviv, Israel
Carlos Rey, Lima, Peru
"Chukie" Salzman, Durban, Natal, South Africa
Luke Van Wyk, Capetown, South Africa
Armando Vignati, Lima Peru
Augusto Wiese, Lima, Peru

PART THREE

SURFING
IN LEGEND
& HISTORY

8. Ancient Surfing Legends

"Ku mai! Ku mai! Ka naru nui nai kahihi!
Alo poi pu. Ku mai Kapohuehue
Hu Kaikooloa."

chanted the ancient Polynesian as he sat with his sporting friends in the shady fern-bordered plateau overlooking their favorite surfing resort. He chanted to his gods, appealing to them for big surf that he and his friends might ride the surging waves, waves first sighted with a feathering crest, waves that shook the very earth when they charged onward to the rugged tropical beach and dashed themselves into glistening spray.

As ancient as legend itself is this appeal directed to the vigorous sporting spirits of the gods of the dim past when there rose mighty men, powerful, but with the gentle desires of children, men who loved the simplicity of nature and spent most of their waking hours in the midst of a paradise not to be surpassed anywhere else in the world. It has been said of a Hawaiian that he is truly happy when he is frolicking in the surf.

To know the story of the origin of the Polynesian is to know the story of the peaceful islands of the Pacific, a conquest by a race of people who are believed to have forced their way from the very heart of Asia, down

119

through the Malay Straits, and across the vast expanses of water, always pushing on toward the rising sun.

This race brought in its veins blood that held deposits of the culture of the East blended with that of the more isolated peaceful peoples who, in the distant past, had settled these contented islands of plenty. Although the ease with which life could be pleasantly sustained contributed to the mellowing of these people, it did not rob them of their vital strength of character and body. They pushed onward with a sureness of purpose that clearly revealed an intelligence far superior to the savages of past ages. In their possession was a culture that eventually left its distinct mark upon all peoples of the great expanse of the Pacific from the South Seas to Hawaii.

As a result a similarity of language, custom, and native legend links all the people of the Polynesian islands into one large South Sea family. We find no trace of legends dealing with surfing prior to the time the Polynesians came to the Hawaiian group. However, it is significant that legends dealing with surfing were contemporary with the earliest legends of the Polynesian when he migrated to Hawaii, indicating that surfing developed after he arrived here.

The sport of surfing was closely associated with the religious life of this ancient people, and, therefore, we find that the surfer who was born to a high social rank engaged in a great deal of sacred ceremony when making his plans to participate in this excellent sport. It was the custom after selecting a suitable tree to make an offering of native *kumu* (fish) at the base of the tree. Then the tree was chopped down and the crude board shaped. After the greater part of trimming and shaping had been accomplished, the board was then taken to the *helau*, or canoe shed, where it was completed. After hours of careful labor it was polished to a great smoothness. The nuts of the *kukui* tree were collected and burned and used to stain the board which was then dedicated with a special prayer and put into use by the surfer.

We have many beautiful legends of these Polynesian people and an extensive number dealing with the sport of surfing. Many of the legends show that the keen competition in the sport led to cruel treatment of the par-

120

Plate 34. San Onofre Beach and surf
taken from the palisade behind the club.

Plate 35. Wind-an-sea Surf, north of
San Diego, California.

By Joe Quigg, Honolulu, Hawaii

ticipants in their quest for a thrill. One of the very earliest legends centers around the present site of the city of Honolulu, the largest and most modern of the island group. Here is the strange story of Mamala, taken from the *Legends of Old Honolulu* by Westervelt.

MAMALA THE SURF-RIDER

"Kou" was the ancient name of Honolulu—the place for games and sports among the chiefs of long ago. A little to the east of Kou and inside the present filled land used for the United States quarantine and coal station was a pond with a beautiful grove of coconut trees belonging to a chief, Hono-kau-pu, afterward known by his name. Straight out toward the ocean was the entrance to the harbor, through which rolled the first surf waves of the Honolulu part of the Island Oahu. The surf bore the name "Ke-kai-o-Mamala"—the "Sea of Mamala." So the sea and entrance to the harbor were known by the name "Mamala," and the shore gave the name "Kou" to the bay.

Mamala was a chiefess of *kupua* character. This meant that she was a *mo-o,* or gigantic lizard or crocodile, as well as a beautiful woman, and could assume whichever shape she most desired. One of the legends says that she was both a shark and woman, and had for her husband the shark-man, Ouha, afterward a shark-god having his home in the ocean near Koko Head. Mamala and Ouha drank *awa* together and played *konane* (a form of checkers) on the smooth *konane* stone at Kou.

Mamala was a wonderful surf-rider. Very skillfully she danced on the roughest waves. The surf in which she most delighted rose far out in the rough sea, where the winds blew strong and whitecaps were on waves which rolled in rough disorder into the bay of Kou. The people on the beach watching her filled the air with resounding applause when they clapped their hands over her extraordinary athletic feats.

The chief, Hono-kau-pu, chose to take Mamala as his wife, so she left Ouha and went to live with her new husband. Ouha was angry and tried at first to injure Hono and Mamala, but he was driven away. He fled to

123

the lake Ka-ihi-Kapu toward Waikiki. There he appeared as a man with a basketful of shrimps and fresh fish, which he offered to the women of that place, saying, "Here is life (a living thing) for the children." He opened his basket, but the shrimps and the fish leaped out and escaped into the water.

The women ridiculed the god-man. The ancient legendary characters of all Polynesia as well as of Hawaii could not endure anything that brought shame and disgrace upon them in the eyes of others. Ouha fled from the taunts of the women, casting off his human form and dissolving his connection with humanity. Thus he became the great god-shark of the coast between Waikiki and Koko Head.

The surf-rider was remembered in the beautiful *mele*, or chant, coming from ancient times and called the *mele* of Hono-kau-pu:

"The surf rises at Koolau,
Blowing the waves into mist,
Into little drops,
Spray falling along the hidden harbor.
There is my dear husband Ouha,
There is the shaking sea, the running sea of Kou,
The crablike, moving sea of Kou.
Prepare the *awa* to drink, the crab to eat.
The small *konane* board is at Hono-kau-pu,
My friend on the highest point of the surf.
There is a good surf for us.
My love has gone away.
Smooth is the floor of Kou,
Fine is the breeze from the mountains.
I wait for you to return,
The games are prepared,
Pa-poko, pa-loa, pa-lele,
Leap away to Tahiti
By the path to Nuumehalani (home of the gods),
Will that lover (Ouha) return?

124

I belong to Hono-kau-pu,
From the top of the tossing surf waves,
The eyes of the day and the night are forgotten.
Kou has the large *konane* board.
This is the day, and to-night
The eyes meet at Kou."

It is very pleasing to note that many legends deal with young women who were remembered for their great skill and grace in handling the surfboard. These ancient women were not afraid of the titanic waves, and we read of how they entered contests with the best of the men of their time, not fearing the threatening sea or the dangers associated with competitive surfing contests where an opponent's board might break away and strike or kill other contestants while it was being heaved and thrown about in the surf.

The following legend, is taken from the book *Legends and Myths of Hawaii by Kalakaua*. It also deals with a woman, a beautiful woman, and shows to what degree the love of this sport controlled this ancient surfing beauty, how she excelled in it in her youth and how, after many years spent away from the surf, she finally returned to this, her first love.

THE LEGEND OF KELEA

There lived at this time at Lihue, Ewa district, Oahu, a chief named Lo-Lale, son of Kalona-iki, and brother of Piliwale, the reigning *Moi* (king) of Oahu. He was a bachelor and a man of an amiable temper. His brothers and friendly neighbouring chiefs became anxious that he should take unto himself a wife. Apparently no suitable match for so high a chief could be found on Oahu, or none had succeeded in captivating the fancy of Lo-Lale. In this case a bride must be sought for abroad, and a proper canoe, with trusty messengers, was fitted out at Waialua to visit the windward islands and report upon the beauty and rank of the chiefesses there. The canoe first visited Molokai, but not satisfied with their inquiries, the messengers proceeded to Lanai, and being equally unsuccessful there, they start-

125

ed to Hana, Maui, intending to cross over to Hawaii. At Hana they learned that Kawaokaohele, the *Moi* of Maui, was at that time stopping with his court and his chiefs at Hamakuapoko, regulating the affairs of the country, and enjoying the cool breezes of that district, and the pleasure of surf-bathing; and that with him was his sister Kelea, the most beautiful woman on Maui and the most accomplished surf-swimmer. Hearing this, the messengers turned back from Hana and arrived with their canoe on a fine morning off Hamakuapoko. On that very morning Kelea and her attendants had gone down to the beach to enjoy the surf-bathing. Swimming out beyond the surf, she encountered the canoe, and was at first somewhat surprised at seeing strangers in it, but being reassured by their kindly speech, and being invited to come on board, the messengers offered to ride the canoe through the surf—a sport as exciting as that of swimming on the surfboard. Kelea accepted the invitation and gallantly the canoe shot over the foaming surf and landed safely on the beach. All sense of danger or mistrust being dispelled, the princess accompanied the canoe again out over the surf, and again rode successfully ashore over the breakers, the attendants hurrahing lustily at the brave and fearless style in which the canoe was handled. The messengers, by this time having ascertained who their illustrious guest was, invited her to another trip through the roaring surf. Thoughtlessly she consented, and the canoe pulled out beyond the surf, watching for a good high combing roller of the sea to start in with. At this moment a squall or a whirlwind suddenly struck the canoe, coming from off the shore, and away it sped with its fair and involuntary passenger over the broad ocean. When the storm had subsided, the shores of Maui were far distant and the messengers started for Waialua, Oahu, where they arrived safely.

From Waialua Kelea was taken up to Lihue, where Lo-Lale received her with the regard due to a chiefess of her rank, and as she did not commit suicide, it may be inferred that she became reconciled to her lot and accepted him as her husband. And as no invasion of Oahu was ever attempted to Kawaokaohele, or vengeance enacted for the abduction of his sister, it is probable, though the legend says nothing about it, that the affair was diplomatically settled to the satisfaction of all parties.

126

Plate 36. Early cigar-box type of hollow board, Hermosa Beach, California.

By Don James, Culver City, California

Plate 37. Left slide at the Cove, Palos Verdes, California.

By Joe Quigg, Honolulu, Hawaii

Plate 38. Pat Patterson with early hollow board during rejuvenation period of surfing activity.

Plate 39. Some early boards, (left to right) laminated balsa, solid balsa and early hollow type boards, Waikiki.

For several years Kelea lived with Lo-Lale at Lihue, and bore to him three children named Kaholi-a-lale, Luli-Wahine, and Luli-Kane. But the inland situation of Lihue, at the foot of the Kaala mountains, and far away from the sea, became wearisome and monotonous to the gay and volatile temper of Kelea. She informed her husband of her intention to leave, and reluctantly he gave his consent, knowing well that the prerogatives of her rank gave her the privilege of separation if she wanted it. His grief at parting has been preserved by the tradition in the form of a chant, the following portion of which alone has been remembered:

Aloha kou hoa i ka puali,
Farewell, my partner on the lowland plains,
I ka wai o pohakea,
On the waters of Pohakea,
He luna o Kanehoa,
Above Kanehoa,
He lae ino o Maunauna
On the dark mountain spur Mauna-una.
O Lihue, he hele ia!
Oh Lihue, she has gone!
Honi aki i ke ala o ka Mauu,
Sniff the sweet scent of the grass,
I ke ala o ke kupukupu,
The sweet scent of the wild vines.
E linoia ana e ka Waikoloa,
That are twisted about by (the brook) Waikoloa
E ka makani he Waiopua-la,
By the winds of Waiopua,
Kuu pu - - - a!
My flower
Me he pula la i kuu maka,
As if a mote were in my eye,
Ka oni i ka haku onohi,
The pupil of my eye is troubled,

131

Ka wailiu I kuu maka. E auwe au-e !

Dimness (covers) my eyes. Woe is me ! Oh !

Leaving Lihue, Kelea descended to Ewa, and skirting the head of the lagoon by way of Halawa, arrived at the mouth of Pearl river opposite Puuloa, and found a crowd of idlers, nobles and retainers of Kalamakua, the high chief of that region, disporting themselves in the surf. Borrowing a surfboard from one of the bystanders, Kelea jumped in the sea and swam out beyond the breakers and joined the company of the other surf bathers. When the surf broke at its highest they all started for the shore, and Kelea excelled them all, and was loudly cheered for her daring and skill. Kalamakua, being at the time in a neighboring plantation heard the loud uproar of voices from the shore, and inquired what the cause of it was. He was told that a beautiful woman from Lihue had beaten all of the Halawa chiefs at surf swimming, and hence the loud and continued cheering. Satisfied in his own mind that but one woman at Lihue could perform such a feat, and that she must be his cousin Lo-Lale's wife, the Maui chiefess, Kalamakua went at once to the beach, and threw his *kihei* (mantle) over Kelea as she touched the shore, returning from another victorious trip through the surf. Explanations followed, and Kelea was borne home in state to the residence of Kalamakua in Halawa, and became his wife. With him she remained to her death, and bore him a daughter, called Laielohelohe, who in early youth was betrothed and subsequently married to her cousin Piilani of Maui, the son of Kelea's brother, Kawaokaohele.

—from *Legends and Myths of Hawaii* by Kalakaua

The inspiration which caused surfing to reach its ultimate pitch of development was the Polynesian desire and delight in gambling. They were great gamblers and would stake their last remaining possession as a wager in a game.

They had plenty of leisure due to the productivity of the islands, and it is only natural that they should look for the most pleasant source of outlet for their energies. They also possessed a keen interest in sports, most of which centered about water. In sporting events, surfing offered the greatest opportunity to the high chiefs because the higher ranking men were always shown preference at surfing locations when the waves were high and the sea was on a rampage. They were the only ones who could afford the ownership and care of superior boards which allow advantage in competition.

Early legends telling of surfing contests are almost entirely built up around petty or ranking chiefs in connection with some particular wager. One of the most interesting deals with a surfing contest in which Umi, a Prince of Hawaii, was a contender.

THE STORY OF UMI

Umi was a very capable lad but also a swaggering, arrogant youngster of royal birth who felt that he could do as he pleased because his father was the king. We find this lack of reasonableness asserting itself unpleasantly in his later years.

Fearing for the safety of his son, the king caused him to travel incognito when touring the island in search of pleasure or adventure. On one of these trips young Umi, a lad of great physical strength, heard of a surfing carnival being held at Laupohoehoe near Hilo on the island of Hawaii. He took his party to Hilo and there haughtily let it be known that he excelled at surfing.

His arrogance was naturally challenged with enthusiasm by one of the petty chiefs, Paeia by name. The wager made was a heavy one calling for four large outrigger canoes (total value of approximately $2,000). But the royal prince treated the wager lightly, meeting it with the assistance of his regal party.

Umi and Paiea paddled out the high surf, pushing their boards through the heavy breakers until they reached the open sea where they spent considerable time maneuvering for the best position. They selected a large wave and paddled madly toward shore. They had chosen the largest wave of the series and it could be seen lifting high into the air, and, at the very crest, throwing spray which was caught by the wind and blown again out to sea. Presently, the force of the wave caught the boards and started them sliding along the slanting surface at the front of the crest.

They both stood up simultaneously, their feet firmly placed on the convex deck of the boards. Magnificent surfers indeed, they were worthy of the keen attention that was given them from the shore by the many observers. They came with great speed and apparently neither surfer experienced difficulty as he glided along the entire course, ending up between the two floats serving as the goal. Umi won the contest and claimed his four canoes, leaving without revealing his identity.

When Umi became king he made a trip to Hilo and caused Paiea to be killed in sacrifice to the gods at the Heiau temple, revengefully claiming that Paiea had allowed his board to bump him slightly while riding beside him in the surfing contest which had been held several years ago.

9. *Historical Notes on Surfing*

It is most unfortunate that recorded history was so late in finding a start in the Polynesian Islands. The people were without a recognized written language of their own until 1821, at which time the missionaries came from Boston and undertook, along with other tasks, the organization of the present Hawaiian language. They published the first schoolbooks and undertook the education of the entire population, wisely using the native language instead of trying to force English upon them.

We do read of early arrivals to the islands before the time of Captain Cook in accounts handed down and repeated to the early explorers. They speak of the arrival of a few oriental people who were absorbed into the race without leaving any trace, and of early Spanish boats driven upon the shores of the islands and wrecked, leaving the few survivors to adjust their lives to that of the natives. One account speaks of the arrival of a white woman, possibly Spanish, who came with several men.

Other Spanish adventurers reported the finding of the islands but did not chart the location correctly, so that the islands were lost again to civilization.

Surprisingly all who came to stay were completely assimilated, leaving

135

no trace of physical characteristics, and more strangely still, leaving no signs of Christianity or of the existing scientific achievements of the time. There was nothing to show that they had made any contribution toward a more advanced form of living. Apparently they all went native and completely forgot the past.

The first authentic discoverer of the islands was Captain Cook of Great Britain who records his adventures in a report to his Majesty, "A Voyage to the Pacific Ocean." None of the sights greeting the captain and his crew created more surprise than the activity of surf swimmers. He speaks of them as showing no fear of water.

It has been said that the babies were taken into the sea the second or third day after birth and, in many cases, they were able to swim as soon as they could walk. To us of the so-called civilized world, taking an infant into the water the second or third day after birth would seem extremely dangerous. But why should it be? The water is warm and the shock is no greater than that experienced by the infant who undergoes the daily bath, powdering, and petting siege. Maybe the natives were not so savage after all in caring for their youngsters when they bathed them in the warm, gentle waters of the Pacific.

Captain Cook spoke of the ease with which the natives swam about and how they were so completely relaxed and happy while in the water, even laughing gayly when overtaken with, what to us, would seem to lead only to tragedy.

This was an accident which he witnessed, and one which clearly showed at what an early age the natives became acclimated to water, losing all fear of it and showing a defiance toward its hazards. He saw a canoe being paddled by a woman who had her children with her. She was paddling near the shore where the breakers heaved and tossed when suddenly a breaker caught her small canoe and threw them all into the sea. One of the children, not over four years of age, was highly pleased and swam about the canoe playing tricks, splashing water and making himself a little pest; and laughing delightedly all the while his mother was setting things in order and getting the children back into the canoe.

136

Our earliest recorded discussion of the white man's reaction to his actual sight of surfing is given by Captain Cook in his report *A Voyage to the Pacific Ocean*, Vol. III. He dramatically reports his entrance into Kealakekua Bay, Hawaii, where he first saw natives riding surfboards, and where coincidentally he met his regrettable death later. His description follows: "Swimming is not only a necessary art in which both their men and women are more expert than any people we had hitherto seen, but a favorite diversion amongst them. One particular mode, in which they sometimes amused themselves with this exercise, in Kealakekua Bay, appeared to us most perilous and extraordinary, and well deserving a distinct relation.

"The surf, which breaks on the coast around the bay, extends to the distance of about one hundred and fifty yards from shore, within which space, the surges of the sea, accumulating from the shallowness of the water, are dashed against the beach with prodigious violence. Whenever, from stormy weather, or any extraordinary swell at sea, the impetuosity of the surf is increased to its utmost height, they choose that time for this amusement which is performed in the following manner: Twenty or thirty of the natives, taking each a long narrow board, rounded at the ends, set out together from shore. The first wave they meet, they plunge under, and suffering it to roll over them, rise again beyond it, and make the best of their way by swimming, out into the sea. The second wave is encountered in the same manner with the first; the great difficulty consisting in seizing the proper moment of diving under it, which, if missed, the person is caught by the surf, and driven back again with great violence; and all his dexterity is then required to prevent himself from being dashed against the rocks. As soon as they have gained, by these repeated efforts, the smooth water beyond the surf, they lay themselves at length on their boards, and prepare for their return. As the surf consists of a number of waves, of which every third is remarked to be always much larger than the others, and to flow higher on the shore, the rest breaking in the immediate space, their first object is to place themselves on the summit of the largest surge, by which they are driven along with amazing rapidity toward the shore. If by mistake they should place themselves on one of the smaller waves, which break before they reach the land, or should not be able to keep their plank in a proper direction on the top of the swell, they are left exposed to the fury of the next, and to avoid it, are obliged again to dive, or regain the place from which they set out. Those who succeed in their object of reaching the shore, have still the greatest danger to encounter. The coast being guarded by a chain of rocks, with, here and there, a small opening between them, they are obliged to steer their board through one of these, or, in case of failure, to quit it, before they reach the rocks, and, plunging under the wave, make the best of their way back again. This is reckoned very disgraceful, and is also attended with a loss of the board, which I have often seen, with great terror, dashed to pieces, at the very moment the islander quitted it. The boldness and address, with which we saw them perform these difficult and dangerous manoeuvres, was altogether astonishing, and is scarce to be credited."

Captain Cook was rightfully known as a man of high ability. He was well educated and possessed a great deal of curiosity. His keen interest in the physical and mental reactions of individuals spoke clearly of his own alertness in observation.

In reading over the great mass of material contained in his report to his sovereign, we detect a definite friendliness toward the native Polynesian. His way of recording incidents seems always to show an understanding of these people and a love for them. One particular incident recorded by him deals with the emotional reaction of the native as he enjoys his water sports. The Captain speaks of it as "the soothing effects produced by particular sorts of motion." However, it seems obviously much more than a "soothing effect." It is perhaps more of a vibrating thrill, although the Captain is correct in that the person is relaxed and quieted following several hours of hard activity in the water.

He gives a splendid report of outrigger canoe surfing, as follows:

"Neither are they strangers to the soothing effects produced by particular sorts of motion, which, in some cases, seem to allay any perturbation of mind, with as much success as music. Of this, I met with a remarkable instance. For on walking, one day, about Natavai Point, where our tents

138

were erected, I saw a man paddling, in a small canoe, so quietly, and looking about with such eagerness, on each side, as to command all my attention. At first, I imagined that he had stolen something from one of the ships, and was pursued; but, on waiting patiently, saw him repeat his amusement. He went out from the shore, till he was near the place where the swell begins to take its rise; and, watching its first motion very attentively, paddled before it, with great quickness, till he found that it overtook him, and had acquired sufficient force to carry his canoe before it, without passing underneath. He then sat motionless, and was carried along at the same swift rate as the wave, till it landed him upon the beach. Then he started out, emptied his canoe, and went in search of another swell.

"I could not help conclude that this man felt the most supreme pleasure while he was driven on, so fast and so smoothly, by the sea; especially as, though the tents and ships were so near, he did not seem in the least, to envy, or even to take any notice of, the crowds of his countrymen collected to view them as objects which were rare and curious. During my stay two or three natives came up, who seemed to share his felicity, and always called out, when there was an appearance of a favorable swell, as he sometimes missed it, by his back being turned, and looking about for it. By then I understood that this exercise which was called *ehorooe* was frequent amongst them; and they have probably more amusements of this sort, which afford them at least as much pleasure as skaiting, which is the only one of ours, with whose effects I could compare it."

ACCOUNTS OF EARLY HISTORIANS

We find the sport of surfing often mentioned by early historians. One, in describing the activity of surfing, writes, "They ride in through the rough sea, into the violent surf at the edge of the beach, making a daring spectacle." He was amused to see natives splashing about, cheering loudly as the surf riders dashed toward the rocks and amazed as he watched them steer their boards around, jump off and catch the board only to climb aboard and repeat the adventure.

139

Almost all of the early writers stressed the native interest in gambling. The surfers would make large personal wagers, and the chiefs who were watching would also gamble on the various contestants. There was always much cheering on shore during the contest.

When the chiefs were surfing, all commoners would keep out of the way. They would gather on the beach and watch with keen interest. It isn't hard to imagine the terrible remorse felt by a high ranking chief if he should handle his board poorly and possibly get dashed against the cliff, resulting in a call for assistance. Because of his high rank, the commoners would not dare jeer at him. The lack of cheering, however, would be silent condemnation.

A cheerful custom, still existent today, was the shouting and cheering of the surfers themselves as they rode through the waves.

We have many records showing the surfing ability of high ranking Polynesians. Kalaimoku, second to the king, prime minister, and high-ranking chief, was a good surfer at the age of sixty years. He was a tremendous man, and must have made a splendid figure, riding his long board toward the shore with the crest of the spray outlining his huge brown form, throwing a white cloud back of him to a height far above his black curly head. He always rode in as a conqueror with his arms crossed in front of him, standing straight and steady on his well-oiled and polished board.

Prince Kauikeaouli (Kamehameha III) was born March 17, 1814, at Keauhou, Hawaii. He was an intrepid surfer and one who often challenged the best surfers of his time. Active and strong with exceptional endurance, he lived on the Big Island (Hawaii), and had a resort house with a broad *lanai* (veranda) located on the beach. He had a stone-bordered grass slide (see Fig. 9) constructed from the beach back into the adjoining hills, upon which he delighted in sliding down on his sled. His favorite pastime was to climb the hills, slide down the grass-covered course to his house, dash in, throw off his clothing, don his *malo* (loin cloth), and take his surf board from the wall. He would run to the water, throw the board onto the surface and spring lightly upon the deck. He would then paddle out to the open sea beyond the rough breakers and wait there for just the particular wave of

140

Fig. 9. Prince Kauikeaouli on his Grass Slide

his fancy. Then, taking a few strong quick strokes, he would spring again to his feet and ride back to the coral beach in front of his house. Kauikeaouli later became King Kamehameha III and ruled until his death.

Another king who was known as the best surfing man of this time was Kaumualii, the ruler of Kauai. Kaumualii was a strong and wise king, and historians of his time mentioned him more frequently than most of the other individuals of his rank. Kaumualii was born in 1778 and was king of the island of Kauai at the time of the conquest of Kamehameha I who conquered all of the islands but Kauai. Kaumualii was too strong for Kamehameha I to conquer. However, through clever scheming, Kamehameha I was able to get him to come to the island of Oahu where he held court, and there he kept Kaumualii under his power, although he did not take his island from him. Kaumualii was known to take a keen interest in the sport of surfing and a number of stories were written about his ability as a surf-rider.

DECLINE OF INTEREST IN SURFING

As previously shown, the ancient Hawaiians spent the greater part of their time at sports, games, and amusements. In this way they kept in excellent physical condition and were, consequently, mentally alert. Sports, particularly water sports, gave them a pleasant relief from the many *kapus*. Outdoor activity kept them in the open and away from a sedentary life, and at the same time made them as cheerful and happy as children. They enjoyed sports that resembled boxing, bowling, coasting, stilt walking, kite flying and top spinning. But of all their ancient sports surfing is the only outstanding one remaining.

The introduction of Christianity into the islands by the Calvinists from Boston in 1821 set into motion a movement so revolutionary and so rigid that almost all of the native customs and activities of these people were submerged. The shock of Christianity and continental civilization so stunned the race that within only a few years the entire population had allowed all their former gods to be destroyed, had broken their taboos, and had been forced by their rulers, who had been converted by the missionaries, to adopt the new life with its busy industrious ideals. They lost the easy life which they had enjoyed for centuries, and were completely overwhelmed by the deluge of civilization.

No time now for idle hours in the shade of the tropical forests. No more time for hours of dancing and feasting on the bounties of nature which were formerly theirs by inheritance. Now life was patterned on a completely new system of taboos. Taboos far greater in number, taboos for which they did not ask and of which they knew nothing. It wasn't necessary to explain. Right was right, and now they must dress in bonnets and wear four petticoats with dark, heavy dresses reaching up to the chin. Tropical heat? No matter, dress they must, and dress they did! Gone were the million delights of contact with nature. Now they must work—farm the soil as it was done in New England. They must make money by being industrious, by working hard, by giving up the pleasure and ease of living. But, why this need of money? They did not want it.

They must give up surfing because it was dimly connected with religious rites of the temple, because it was wrong to gamble. All this had suddenly become wrong and would not fit into the new pattern of life. The rigid, iron-willed courage, and stamina of the Calvinists of the first deluge, shocked and stunned the Polynesians into a state that caused them to forget completely their past pleasures, almost forget the past pleasure of surfing.

We find that missionaries forced clothing upon the surfer so that he no longer surfed with his *malo* (loin cloth). Now he must battle the waves, hindered by the moral disapproval of such a waste of time, plus the added handicap of pants and shirt as well as a good whaling with the butt of a cane stalk when he returned to his school or household.

Surf-riding experienced a steady decline from 1821 until 1900, at which time it was practically a memory. The only semblance remaining was the sight of a few lads floating about occasionally on old planks close to the beach. It speaks well for the fiber and value of surfing as a sport to note it took some seventy-nine years to get it discouraged or suppressed. One writer reports that in 1853 only one place existed where surfing was main-

143

tained with any degree of enthusiasm. The spot was Lahaina on the island of Maui.

Only strong men who were fired with a purpose could continue to surf at Hawaii or at the many former surfing centers, and now that gambling was no longer allowed, there was little reason to show a keen interest. Maui and Oahu enjoyed calmer seas, and surfing in these places was not as hazardous as on the other islands. One missionary in making his report mentioned that some of the children would occasionally take a "try at the board, but usually would get whacked about with the waves," probably with no more harm than the whaling received upon the arrival home.

Not wishing to have the readers organize and storm the first missionary hut, it may be best to hasten and say in their defense that much good came from the influx of civilized living standards. It is pleasing to note that each deluge of missionaries brought more liberal ideals and today the descendants of these staunch families are as loyal to Hawaii as the first Polynesian who luckily drifted upon these coral shores.

REJUVENATION OF SURFING ACTIVITY

The period of rejuvenation of surfing activity dates from 1900. At that not distant period, surfers were splashing about on boards usually of a nondescript type averaging approximately six to seven feet in length.

The great athletic era was well under way all over the world at the turn of the century, and it is only natural that this exceptional activity should again recover its breath and fall in line with the general march toward better living and better care of the physical body, so long neglected because of the religious fever which had blazed so many years and was just burning itself out.

Surfing first showed its proof of rebirth by a general lengthening of the surfboards put into use. In 1910 we therefore find boards measuring from eight to ten feet appearing on the heretofore nearly deserted surf reefs. The youngsters were becoming more interested in this grand sport, and were reaching out toward the higher waves where only a few years before,

144

very few ventured. They now needed larger boards, and as a result an improvement in board construction was seen.

To speak of the revival of surfing activity without mentioning Lorrin Thurston, Duke Kahanamoku, and Dad Center would show a lack of appreciation for their noteworthy contribution to this sport. Thurston was one of the first to lengthen his boards to twelve feet. None of the waves came too big or too rough for these pioneers.

By the early twenties, quite a few island youngsters were showing an increasing interest in the sport, with the result that tourists from the mainland were also attracted to the activity, and many of them became staunch supporters of and participants in the sport.

With the spread of surfing interest into the mainland and Australia, we find some interesting and unusual results. On the Pacific Coast where there were no coral reefs to throw up a consistent surf, many adopted the sport only to paddle about in the open sea and only a few were adventurous enough to make a try at surfing in the breakers. In Australia, where the breakers are quite different from Hawaii, surfers were riding the waves after they had broken, and they were not standing on the boards. They developed a different board, one that appears more like a very shallow canoe, using small wooden paddles. They also developed a shorter and wider board, mostly enjoying the sport by paddling about as they did in California.

Some years went by—paddling. However, these years were not wasted because the coast lads were constantly improving their boards. They first developed the balsa board and followed that with the development of the hollow paddle board which is excellent for racing. These lads developed such a keen interest in paddling that they still hold races between the California coast and Santa Catalina Island, a distance of more than twenty-one miles.

The development of the lighter boards constructed of balsa wood, and of the hollow type of board, gave a new impetus to the sport of surfing. The beginner could now paddle about with good speed and could occasionally catch a lucky ride, when heretofore he could not make any headway through the water and had great difficulty in balancing on the older types of boards. Surfing immediately took its rightful place and has since shown a constant increase in Hawaii, on the Pacific Coast and in Australia. Many locations have been discovered in all of these countries; and again surfing has become one of the world's most thrilling sports!

Appendix

HAWAIIAN EQUIVALENTS OF WESTERN NAMES

MEN

Abraham, Aberehama
Alexander, Alika
Alfred, Alapaki
Andrew, Aneru
Anthony, Akoni
Antonio, Akoni
Arthur, Aka

Barney, Bane
Benedict, Benekiki
Benjamin, Beniamina
Bernard, Belenaka

Calvin, Kalawina
Carl, Kala

Charles, Kale
Clarence, Kalalena
David, Kawiki
Donald, Donala

Earl, Ele
Edward, Eluwene
Eric, Elika
Ernest, Eneki

Frank, Palakiko
Fred, Peleke

George, Keoki
Gerald, Gerala

Harold, Hale

Isaac, Aikake

Jack, Keaka
Jacob, Jakobo
James, Iakopo
Jim, Kimo
John, Keoni

Kenneth, Keneke

Lawrence, Lapaki
Leo, Lio
Lewis, Lui
Lincoln, Linekona

Mark, Mareko
Michael, Mikaele

Milton, Milikona
Moses, Moke

Nathan, Natana
Norman, Nomana

Oliver, Oliwa

Patrick, Palika
Paul, Paulo
Peter, Petero
Phillip, Pilipo

Ralph, Rala
Richard, Likelike

Samuel, Kamuela
Simon, Kimona

Theodore, Teo
Thomas, Kamaki

Victor, Viki
Vincent, Vikeni

Walter, Wala
William, Williama

WOMEN

Adele, Akela
Agnes, Akaneki
Angela, Anakela

Alice, Alika

Barbara, Babara
Beatrice, Bikale
Bertha, Peke
Betty, Bete
Blanche, Balaniki

Carol, Kalole
Catherine, Kakalina
Clara, Kalala
Cynthia, Kinikia

Deborah, Kapule
Diana, Kina
Dolores, Dolore
Dorothy, Kaloke

Edith, Edi
Edna, Edena
Elizabeth, Elikapeka
Elsie, Elese
Emily, Emele
Ethel, Ekela

Florence, Felorena
Frances, Palani

Gertrude, Gerekuke
Gladys, Gladi
Grace, Lokomaikai

Harriet, Hariaka

Helen, Helena

Ida, Ida
Irene, Irene

Jane, Kini
Janet, Ianete
Joan, Ioana
Josephine, Kepina

Katherine, Kakalina

Laura, Lola
Lillian, Liliana
Lois, Loika
Louise, Luika
Lucy, Luke

Mabel, Mapela
Margaret, Makaleka
Marion, Mariana
Mary, Mele
Mildred, Milikeke

Nancy, Ane
Nora, Nora

Olive, Olivia

Pearl, Momi
Phyllis, Pilisi

Rachel, Rahela

Rosalie, Lokalia
Rose, Loke
Ruth, Luka

Sara, Kalai
Susan, Suke

Sylvia, Silivia

Teresa, Teresa
Thelma, Kama

Victoria, Wikolia

Vialet, Waioleka
Virginia, Viviana

Wilma, Wilima
Winifred, Winepeleke

SOME COMMON HAWAIIAN WORDS

Alii, a chief; nobleman
Aloha, greeting; hello; farewell
Au, to swim
Auwe, woe; alas

Ehu, red
Ewa, direction of Honolulu

Haina, to tell
Hale, house
Hana, to word
Haole, foreign to Hawaii
Heenalu, surfboarding
Heiau, temple
Hiamoe, to sleep
Hoku, a star; high
Holo, rubbing; sailing
Holoku, a loose dress
Honi, a kiss
Hoolaulea, make merry
Hoomalimali, to flatter
Huhu, angry
Hui, assembly; group
Hukilau, method of fishing

Hula, to dance
Huli, to turn

Iki, small
Ilio, a dog
Imu, underground oven
Ipo, sweetheart

Kai, the sea
Kala, dollar; money
Kalo, taro plant
Kamaaina, child of the land
Kane, man; male person
Kapu, prohibited; keep out
Kau, summer season
Kauka, doctor
Kaukau, food; to eat
Kea, white in color
Keiki, offspring; first-born
Ko, sugar cane
Kokua, to help
Kona, the south
Kope, coffee
Kukui, nut-bearing tree

149

Kumu, a fish

Moana, ocean

La, the sun
Lama, torch ; light
Lamalama, to fish with a torch
Lanai, a bower, porch
Lani, the sky
Laulau, food in a bundle
Lei, ornamental pieces for head or neck
Lio, the horse
Lolo, stupid ; ignorant
Lomilomi, massage ; to rub
Luau, a feast

Mahalo, thank you (gracious form)
Mai, comely
Maia, banana
Makai, toward the sea
Make, to die ; dead
Malama, take care of ; watch over
Malihini, newcomer
Malo, loin cloth
Mauka, toward the mountains
Mele, song
Menehune, legendary race of dwarfs

Nani, beautiful ; splendid
Nui, big ; large

Okolehao, liquor from ti root
Oli, chant ; sing
Onaona, beautiful ; attractive odor
Opu, the abdomen

Pake, Chinese
Palapala, printing ; book
Pali, precipice
Panini, cactus
Paniolo, cowboy
Pau, finished
Pilau, stench ; stink
Pilikia, trouble
Puka, entrance ; hole
Pupule, insane

Waa, canoe
Wahine, a female
Wai, water ; liquids
Wikiwiki, to hasten ; hurry